FRANZ BARDON: QUESTIONS & ANSWERS AND THE GREAT ARCANUM

Compiled from the Teachings of
Franz Bardon

By
Dieter Rüggeberg

Answers to 185 of the Most Frequently
Asked Spiritual Questions
Including 9 Charts of Virtues and Passions
As they Pertain to the Four Elements

2013
Merkur Publishing, Inc.
Wisdom of the Occident

About Franz Bardon
(1909-1958)

With permission from Divine Providence, the spirit of a highly developed Hermetic adept entered the body of a fourteen-year-old child named Franz Bardon, destined to become one of the most remarkable magicians of the 20th century.

Though he maintained a "normal life" as an industrial mechanic and family man in the Czech town of Opava, his other, occult life was full of attainment, power and tragedy.

During the last years of WWII, Franz Bardon spent three and a half months in a concentration camp, from which he ultimately escaped. After the war, he practiced as a naturopath and graphologist and devoted himself to the teaching of Hermeticism and the writing of his now classic works, *Initiation into Hermetics*, *The Practice of Magical Evocation*, and *The Key to the True Kabbalah*.

This newly discovered work will help students of Hermetics with precise information on universal principles.

© 2008 Dieter Rüggeberg

All rights reserved. No part of this book may be reproduced, stored in a mechanical retrieval system, or transmitted in any form by electronic, video, laser, mechanical, photocopying, recording means or otherwise, in part or in whole, without the express written consent of the publisher, except for brief quotations embodied in critical articles for review.

First English Edition 2008
Second Printing 2009
Third Printing 2013
ISBN 9781885925191

Translated by permission from the German original *Fragen an Master Arion (Franz Bardon)* © 1997 Dieter Rüggeberg and *Hermetische Psychologie und Charakterkunde* © 2004 Verlag Dieter Rüggeberg

Translated by Gerhard Hanswille and Franca Gallo

Printed in the United States of America

Merkur Publishing, Inc.
PO Box 171306
Salt Lake City UT
USA 84117

www.merkurpublishing.com

CONTENTS

Foreword	7
Questions and Comments Concerning the Mental Plane	9
Questions Concerning the Astral Plane	27
Questions Concerning the Physical Plane	39
The Function of the Akasha	53
Foreword to the Great Arcanum	61
Chart 1: Fire Element (Jod י in Hebrew)	64
Chart 2: Air Element (He ה in Hebrew)	65
Chart 3: Water Element (Vau ו in Hebrew)	66
Chart 4: Earth Element (He ה in Hebrew)	67
Chart 5: A. Principles and Ideas (Akasha)	68
Chart 6: B. Fire Element	70
Chart 7: C. Air Element	76
Chart 8: D. Water Element	88
Chart 9: E. Earth Element	100

Foreword

The manuscript for this little book was prepared in Prague by a group of Franz Bardon's students, probably in the early 1950s, when Bardon's books, *Initiation into Hermetics*, *The Practice of Magical Evocation* and *The Key to the True Kabbalah*, had not yet been published. Mr. Jonny Schwartz received the original from Mrs. Irina Novakova and was kind enough to allow me to publish it, for which I am very grateful.

I would also like to extend my gratitude to Dr. M. K. and to Silvia and Ulrich Ohm, who edited and corrected the original German manuscript. May students of Hermetics find encouragement and inspiration for the practical part of their work herein. Every practitioner knows how difficult it is to express spiritual experiences in words. The principal reason for publishing this work is to provide inspiration for students of Hermetics in their meditative exercises.

Wuppertal, April 1997
Dieter Rüggeberg

Notes to the Reader

1. To fully appreciate the information contained in this booklet, it is imperative that students of the occult sciences become familiar with Franz Bardon's series of books on Hermetics. The first volume, *Initiation into Hermetics*, deals with the theory and practice of the Hermetic arts. The second volume, *The Practice of Magical Evocation*, continues along the Hermetic path with a description of the various planetary spheres and beings, while *The Key to the True Kabbalah* deals with the ancient science of sacred sound and the word. The information contained in this present work should be a welcome addition to the Bardon books because it answers the questions most frequently asked by students, and also clarifies many statements in the earlier books.

2. The term "the exercises" mentioned throughout this work refers to "Hermetic exercises."

Questions and Comments Concerning the Mental Plane

1. *What is the will?*

The will is a fundamental attribute of the spirit; it is an aspect of the universal Fire element. As a quality, the will expresses itself only in the content or goal of the wish. Most of us simply make an effort and wish to attain something, but we do not possess the right power to make that wish manifest. That is why we continue to wish.

The power of the will is the quantity through which we achieve, produce, carry out and maintain what we aim for and what we wish for.

2. *What is belief?*

Belief is a quality. In general, its foundation is a particular belief, whether in the existence of God or of something else. The quantity of a manifested belief is a power that expresses itself in an absolute and unshakable conviction that what we believe in will positively become a reality. Belief as a power is a complement; it is the organ that bears the impulsive part of the will. The manifested belief is the highest aspect of the Akasha principle.

3. *Aspects of the intellect and intelligence, memory and discernment. The ability to recognize and differentiate.*

Intellect or intelligence is a fundamental attribute of the eternal spirit. It is an aspect of the universal Air element on the mental plane. Intelligence or intellect can be measured and is therefore quantitative. Through it we understand, recognize, differentiate, judge and remember everything.

The quality of the intellect, intelligence, is the substance (content) which the intellect works on. Generally, it has its physical seat in the chest, where the Air element is located and where it is at work. In accordance with Indian philosophy, the seat of the intellect, together with the will, is in the head, between the eyebrows, in the astral body. Memory is an aspect of the intellect. Its quality is the substance (thoughts, events, pictures, impressions, perceptions etc.) which it draws from its reserves.

4. *What are feelings, life and love?*

Feelings, life and love are all aspects of the universal Water element as a fundamental attribute of the eternal spirit on the mental plane. Feeling is a quality that expresses itself in pleasant, unpleasant, ugly, pure and many other feelings. Its quantity, for example, is the aggregate of normal feelings which are controlled by the will, or passionate, uncontrolled, quick or very weak, hardly perceptible feelings. It expresses itself on all planes depending on the content and the power of the effect.

Life is the result of the work of the elements in the tetrapolar magnet on all planes. The qualitative life reflects in a human being through polarized radiation of the elementary attributes. For the astral plane, see information on the aura (pp. 16, 20, 28). Qualitative life expresses itself in the temporary (i.e. in a particular length of time):

a. in time and space on the material plane,
b. in space on the astral plane, and
c. in eternity, without time and space, on the mental plane.

Life expresses itself in any type of activity or movement that can be measured.

Love is a universal law. In order to be recognized by His created beings, God divided Himself on His highest level of love into a plus and a minus. This means that He divided everything created into something active and passive, positive and negative, through which an absolute, unalterable lawfulness came into existence.

Love is quantity, because it can be measured. Through love we express our positive relationship for everything we like and love. True love must be controlled by the will. Passions can originate from an uncontrolled love, which means passionate love, for example sexual love, which originates from a fiery sensual love, or an abnormal love of wealth, of animals, parents, children, husband or wife. But it can also be the uncontrolled love for God Himself, as for instance among the mystics.

Love controlled by the will protects us from any overwrought state, and we express our love, of whatever kind it might be, in a form that corresponds to our power and perception of what the object of our love deserves. It is of course a foregone conclusion that we love our Creator above all. That is the highest, purest and mightiest love.

The quality of love as an attribute expresses itself in its rays, in its polarity and in its various kinds.

5. *What is the instinct of self-preservation?*

The instinct of self-preservation is the lowest aspect of the Akasha principle. It exists on every plane in accordance with circumstances and causes. Its power or quantity is that much greater the more the life of a human being is threatened, as for example in the case of fatal diseases, serious accidents, war and so on.

The value of the quality of the instinct of self-preservation lies in the wish to live as long as possible on the material plane. We may assign this instinct for self-preservation to the active attributes and powers whenever the person concerned applies it for noble purposes and to the negative attributes and powers whenever a person wants to prolong his life simply for egotistical reasons.

6. What are self-consciousness and the "I" consciousness?

Self-consciousness is a state in which we become conscious of who we are. This consciousness signifies that we identify ourselves in the mental sphere with the highest divine idea, with the eternal spirit that exists within us.

The *"I" consciousness* is a fundamental attribute of the spirit on the mental plane as an aspect of the universal Earth element. It is also a mirror of our active attributes. In the thought, its qualitative part appears to us as active. The "I" consciousness contains all the fundamental attributes of the spirit, the Fire, Air and Water elements which are the will, intellect and feelings, love and life. It is effective in the entire body and as an energy; it is the quantitative part of the consciousness and is also contained in the blood. The consciousness of the cerebrum is located on the mental plane, in the mental body.

7. What is the subconscious?

The subconscious is the mirror of all our negative attributes and is located in the interbrain in the astral body. The uncontrolled subconscious is our enemy. It is especially effective at night, in space without time, when the body and the normal consciousness are at rest. We can control our subconscious through autosuggestion if we order it to do something good for us just before we fall asleep. We assign the subconscious to our storehouse of ideas where it exists as a qualitative component. Its quantity is the power of the effect and tension of the opposite negative attributes.

8. The elements outside time and space and their effects.

Among the five elements, we must differentiate the four that have originated from the highest, mightiest, most incomprehensible and indefinable element, the Akasha. These are the four universal elements: Fire, Air, Water and Earth. Every element has two poles, active and passive or positive and negative.

The attributes and powers of the elements are also known to us individually from the tetrapolar magnet. Fire, Air, Water and Earth are effective as universal elements without time and space on the mental plane. The Akasha principle is effective as the eternal Ether, the causal world, without time and space on all planes. It contains everything created, therefore also the tetrapolar magnet, the electromagnetic fluid which is the highest universal law of the macro- and microcosm. The primordial ideas or primary elements are primordial qualities which, through the corresponding power of a wish, also contain quantity. Akasha is both quality and quantity.

9. What is mental asceticism?

Mental asceticism means the observance of decency and discipline, order and purity, control of all thoughts, images, and impressions which reach our consciousness from the causal world by means of the mental matrix; in order to achieve this, we make use of our will.

10. What is thinking?
Thinking is both quality and quantity. It divides into two parts: our normal consciousness, which is the active part, and our subconscious, which is the passive part. Both the consciousness and the subconscious contain the qualities of thinking, whose quantity is increased through the exertion of one's powers.

11. What is knowledge and what is wisdom?
Knowledge is an active attribute of the Air element which *is dependent* upon intelligence, intellect, memory, mental receptivity, talent, maturity, recognition and discernment, regardless of whether we obtain our knowledge theoretically or through practical experiences.

Wisdom is also an attribute of the universal Air element, but is *not dependent* upon memory, intellect, intelligence and knowledge, although knowledge and wisdom are to a certain degree identical.

The source of wisdom is within God, in the causal principle, on all planes of the Akasha. Wisdom is dependent upon the recognition, maturity, perfection, purity and noble-mindedness of the individual. We attain wisdom through inspiration and intuition. Our degree of wisdom indicates our level of development. Knowledge and wisdom are directed mainly towards recognition of all the laws of the macro- and microcosm, primarily on the part of wisdom and from an intellectual point of view, or, in other words, in bipolar fashion. Wisdom and knowledge can be measured and hence are also quantitative. Their quality expresses itself in results.

12. What is a manifested state of belief?
A manifested state of belief is a firm and absolute conviction that becomes reality: it is whatever we envision and create through the power of our will and our imagination.

The will is electric and has its opposite procreative pole in manifested belief, which can move mountains.

By means of these two principles, the electric and magnetic fluids, everything was created. If we want to acquire creative power and willpower, imagination and manifested belief, we must identify ourselves with the Akasha principle, which exists in us as an eternal spirit.

A manifested state of belief can be measured in accordance with one's degree of development and maturity, for example the healing of the woman who believed that she would get well as soon as she touched the garment of Master Jesus.

13. The difference between recognition and conviction.

We acquire knowledge through recognition; through conviction (manifested belief) we secure our belief that this recognition is in reality lawful and true. General recognition is quality. Inner recognition, depth, the core of every created matter, the recognition directed upon every being, represents the power of recognition (quantity). Conviction is an aspect of belief that is connected with absolute truth and lawfulness.

When we recognize something, we make use of all our external senses and, when necessary, we also use our internal senses. Recognition is an aspect of the Air element. Conviction originates from our belief, which directly reflects itself in the Akasha principle.

14. What is chaos and what is harmony?

Chaos is a particular negative state (disharmony) which originates from the lawfulness of the negative directions, in opposition to harmony. Harmony is the congruity of all lawfulness that is effective in the entire universe in the positive or negative sense. We observe that everything created is linked together in congruity with absolute precision, just like the wheels in a clock. If chaos comes into being somewhere, it is immediately offset in a natural and lawful manner.

Chaos and harmony are attributes; they are qualities of the present. Their quantities depend in the case of chaos upon the power of disagreement, and in the case of harmony upon the guiding power, the Akasha principle.

15. What are larvae, elementals, and elementaries?

A larva may be either a mental or an astral being, but usually it is an astral being created through constant repetition of an intensive thought. It is mostly connected with a particular passion or bad habit or with other negative attributes. A person usually creates these beings unknowingly from a mental or astral substance in the mental or astral matrix.

A larva is actually a half-being that lives on the lowest plane of the mental or astral worlds. Depending on where it lives, it may nourish itself with either mental or astral substances stemming from the particular passion or negative attribute out of which it was created. It has a form or shell in accordance with its attribute, and also a strong instinct for self-preservation. On the path of Hermetics, a strongly developed larva is usually a very difficult obstacle to overcome. A person creates larvae when he fails to control his negative attributes. He becomes surrounded by a whole swarm of such larvae, which constantly prepare favorable opportunities for him to arouse the passion through which they nourish themselves at his expense.

An elemental is a being created from a mental substance in the mental matrix by a human being, a magician. Depending upon the purpose for which this being is created, the magician creates the elemental out of particular elements and gives it form and attributes in accordance with its tasks. He gives it a piece of his own consciousness; he gives it a name and determines its life span; he gives it a task and then detaches himself from it. Since the elemental cannot form an astral shell, it lives and works on the mental plane. When it works, it nourishes itself from the mental substance of its creator. If it is to work on behalf of other human beings, the energy can be taken from the universe. As a rule, an elemental has only one attribute and performs one single task. The elemental cannot fulfill any tasks for which the magician himself does not have the capabilities.

An elementary is an astral being that is also created by a magician. As a rule, it is created consciously out of a particular element, from the astral substance of the astral matrix. It is provided with one or more attributes and is endowed with a part of its creator's consciousness. Furthermore, it possesses a name and a particular form, and its life span is predetermined. The magician charges the elementary with several tasks; after these tasks have been fulfilled, the elementary usually dissolves itself into the original astral substance from which it was created. It lives solely on the astral plane and nourishes itself from the astral substance of its creator and has a very strong instinct for self-preservation. As a rule it is intelligent, and has a tendency to become independent if the magician fails to keep it firmly under his will and control. Therefore it is vitally important that every elementary be limited to a particular time as far as its life span is concerned, which means that it has to be given strict orders to dissolve itself completely after it has fulfilled its task. Otherwise this being may cause all kinds of mischief at the expense of its creator, and the creator will be responsible.

16. *Methods to improve the will, belief and intellect.*
We can improve the will, belief and intellect through autosuggestion. We can also strengthen the will with visual, acoustic, perceptual, taste and olfactory exercises. The will is also strengthened through asceticism, magical prayer, and introspection — through continuous battle against negative attributes until complete mastery over them is achieved — and by surmounting any obstacles during the exercises and also in all other possible cases.

We strengthen our belief through consciousness when we carry out all our magical exercises and labors as an eternal spirit rather than in ordinary human fashion; through this we imitate God Himself in His creative activities. We consciously place ourselves in the proper mood through a prayer, a gesture or something similar, and by so doing we place ourselves into a half-trance. We also strengthen our belief through successes and through the verification of particular truths.

We improve the intellect through diligent study of the universal laws, meditation, recognition, the ability to differentiate, and through general education and knowledge. This leads to the ennobling and perfection of the spirit, soul and body, which is further achieved through the connection of our consciousness with our guardian spirit and with the Akasha principle or the intelligences that belong to it, through inspiration and intuition as the result of profound meditation, and also through the exercises with the universal Air element and the universal eternal light, which are endowed with immeasurable, incomprehensible intelligence.

17. *How do we expand our consciousness?*
We expand our consciousness through techniques that include all the optical, acoustic and perceptual exercises. We can also expand and strengthen our consciousness through autosuggestion, meditation and prayer.

18. *What differences exist in the effects of the elements on the mental plane?*
On the mental plane the elements are effective without time and space. As long as we are dealing with thought formations, abstract thoughts or plastic images with a single idea, these are charged through the Fire element with pure electric fluid. They are pure electric thoughts. When it comes to the Water element, we are dealing with pure magnetic thoughts; when it comes to the Air element, we are dealing with pure neutral thoughts; and when it comes to the Earth element, we are dealing with thoughts with pure electromagnetic fluid.

In general, the Fire element is effective on the mental plane expansively; it produces heat and light. The Water element expresses itself through the opposite attributes: constriction, coldness and darkness. Air neutralizes and balances the effects of Fire and Water and Earth solidifies; Earth consolidates the other three elements and limits their effect. Besides that, Earth is accentuated through the tetrapolar magnet, the electromagnetic fluid.

On the highest aspects of the mental plane, a human being can achieve omnipotence and all-encompassing primordial powers through the Fire element; omniscience, purity, clarity and lawfulness through the Air element; love and eternal life through the Water element; and immortality and omnipresence — in other words, eternity — through the Earth element.

Also, the fundamental attributes of the eternal spirit correspond on the mental plane with the different activities of the elements:

> Fire corresponds to the will;
> Air corresponds to intellect, intelligence;
> Water corresponds to feelings, life, love; and
> Earth corresponds to consciousness.

19. *How do the electric and magnetic fluids differ in their effects on the mental plane?*
The electric fluid causes expansion, heat and light on the mental plane, whereas the magnetic fluid causes the opposite — constriction, cold and darkness. The electric

fluid fills abstract thoughts with pure electric fluid, warmth, expansion and dynamics. The magnetic fluid fills them with pure magnetic fluid and the opposite attributes.

For example, the electric fluid expresses itself through its attributes in willpower, while the magnetic fluid expresses itself in the antipole of the will, that is, in manifested belief, an aspect of the productive universal power. We also see the electric fluid in constant active action, vigor and movement, in creative activities, in revolutionary development and discharge.

On the mental plane, the magnetic fluid expresses itself in the opposite attributes, in evolution and eternal rest.

20. What is the power of the imagination?
The power of the imagination is an attribute, a quality through which we imagine alive[1] visually, acoustically, perceptively or all together, as well as through taste, smell, some kind of circumstance, a person, being, idea, topic, thought, picture, quality and attribute of a matter etc. This applies especially to the exercises, but also to everyday life. The quantity of the imagination expresses itself in the intensification, lessening and waning of the imagination.

21. The difference between an imagination and an elemental.
An imagination is a true image of what we imagine; reality is that which we create with the help of the will, concentration, the power of the imagination and manifested belief respectively.

In contrast to this, an elemental is a being that we create in a magical manner from the mental substance and from particular elements and which we provide with a name. This being has a part of our consciousness, carries out certain tasks, has an instinct for self-preservation, and nourishes itself from the mental substance which we emanate into the mental world, consciously draw from, and also give to the universe.

22. With what does the mental body nourish itself?
The mental body nourishes itself with thoughts from the mental plane and with pictures and impressions with the help of the senses.

23. How does the spirit express himself in the astral world and in the material plane?
The spirit expresses himself in the astral world through his astral body, the soul, and with his attributes and powers in the tetrapolar magnet. On the material plane, the spirit expresses himself through the astral matrix, out of which the soul emanates in various colors in accordance with the polarity of the effects of the elements.

---

[1] As opposed to dead – ED.

This emanation of the attributes is called the aura, which at the same time exposes the fundamental character of a human being in accordance with the elements.

On the material plane, the spirit expresses himself through his material body with all the functions of the elements that are identical with the functions of the astral body. For the most part, these are the attributes analogous to the effects of all the elements in the tetrapolar magnet, through which the spirit expresses himself on the material plane in time and space.

24. What are concentration, meditation, fixation, contemplation and fantasy?

Concentration is an uninterrupted hold or adherence to a point, matter, being, abstract concept, idea, picture, thought, perception etc. Concentration is divided into three levels in accordance with periods of time. The first level is an uninterrupted concentration of twelve seconds and is called *dharana*. The second level, *dhyana*, has a duration of twelve times twelve seconds, while the third level has a duration of twelve times twelve times twelve seconds and is called *samadhi*, which means ecstasy, the flowing together of subject and object.

Meditation serves the purpose of disassembling or analyzing a matter, an abstract concept, an idea, thought, picture etc., in all its aspects and details, and also analyzing the matter on all planes in the well known manner — with the will, the intellect and the feelings (analysis).

Fixation is the exact measuring, stabilization and uninterrupted holding onto of a particular object, thought, point etc., during concentration.

Contemplation is the consideration or reflection upon and analysis of a particular object, matter, idea, being, picture, impression, thought and its attributes in the different spheres. For example, if we want to be certain that a picture or an object is real, we first look at it with open eyes and then with our eyes closed. If the picture does not change and disappear, it is a reality; if otherwise, it is a delusion.

Fantasy is often ignited through the beauty of an object; it has a stimulating effect upon our senses, and this is increased through various stimuli. Fantasy always has a personal, subjective, relative, and individual coloration and direction in accordance with mood and temper.

25. What can be substituted in place of the exercises?

We can substitute meditation, autosuggestion, belief, prayer, introspection, noble deeds, asceticism, wisdom, knowledge, silence, love and humility in place of the exercises.

26. What purpose do the exercises serve?

We ennoble, perfect and strengthen our spirit, soul and physical body through the exercises. Most of all, we strengthen all the active (positive) attributes and powers of all the universal elements which work in and around us. Through the exercises we realize divine ideas in and around us, beginning with the lowest and progressing to the highest, until we become one with God.

27. How is the Akasha principle effective on the mental plane?
On the mental plane, the Akasha principle is effective as the causal world without time and space. It is the highest, most incomprehensible power; although uncreated, it created everything and also guides everything.

In a human being, the Akasha principle appears on the mental plane as the highest, most leading and guiding principle, as well as in the mental matrix and in the consciousness; it also appears as the controlling divine principle of the conscience as it pertains to intuition, inspiration, belief and the instinct for self-preservation. The Akasha principle is an obstacle on the path of our exercises on the mental plane through thoughts, pictures and imagination, which of course disturb our exercises, but which on the other hand strengthen our will.

The mental matrix is the finest substance of the spiritual Akasha principle. It connects the mental body with the astral body and transfers all thoughts, plastic pictures, and impressions to the consciousness of the spirit. The Akasha principle expresses itself on the mental plane in electric, magnetic, electromagnetic and indifferent neutral thoughts. In thoughts, you find fundamental ideas that originated in the causal world of the Akasha principle. The Akasha principle works by means of these ideas through thought upon our consciousness and subconscious, through which these ideas are accepted and processed, realized or refused.

28. What is the purpose of fate on the mental plane?
All thoughts, pictures, impressions, etc., that belong as causes on the mental plane enter and register themselves carefully and precisely in the causal world on the mental plane. In accordance with their inner value, they can form positive or negative effects or consequences that belong to them and are lawful, and which of course have a tremendous influence upon the character (attributes) of a person.

The reminiscences or reflections and effects return to a person to ennoble him when he is positive; when he is negative, they attack him until he has equilibrated his errors and their causes.

29. What is the difference between spiritual maturity and a high development of the spirit?
A mature spirit has reached the level of recognition and conviction. He has become a part of the divine principle and he searches for means and sources in order to identify himself with this, the highest divine principle. A highly developed spirit has already

identified himself with the divine principle, and continues on the path of the highest ennoblement and perfection.

30. How do the mental and astral materia effect the spiritual senses?
The mental and astral materia are effective through impressions (perceptions) upon the spiritual senses, which reach the consciousness of the spirit from all planes by means of the mental matrix. In the mental matrix they are effective without being limited to time and space; on the astral plane they are effective in space.

The spirit processes these impressions with the help of the elementary functions of the tetrapolar magnet in the mental and astral bodies.

31. What is the mental matrix and what is its function?
The mental matrix or, rather, the tetrapolar magnet is a connecting link between the mental and astral bodies; it is the finest spiritual Akashic substance that guides the functions of the spirit. It is created from the finest spiritual Akashic substance that exists in the human body. The mental matrix or ethereal principle, transfers all thoughts, pictures and impressions from all planes to the consciousness of the spirit with the help of the material, astral and spiritual senses. The spirit then processes these impressions with the help of the astral and physical bodies.

32. Methods with which fantasy can be enhanced.
Fantasy can be enhanced through particular stimulants or excitants, by raising one's thoughts and feelings, through beauty, music, nature, song, love, fragrances, incense, and so on.

33. What kind of attributes does the mental matrix have?
The mental matrix has the attributes of the tetrapolar magnet and guides the activity of the spirit in the astral body. The mental matrix is electromagnetic and guides thoughts and the imagination to the consciousness of the spirit. The mental matrix connects the mental body with the astral body.

34. What purpose does the mental matrix serve?
The mental matrix as the tetrapolar magnet is the center of all attributes and powers of the eternal spirit, which makes use of them in the astral body, which is his shell. After the eternal spirit leaves his two shells — that is, the material body and the astral body — the mental matrix keeps all the attributes and powers which the person possessed at the end of his material life on earth and takes them with him into the mental plane.

35. What is the difference between an idea and a thought?

A human being can either find an idea by himself, or he can acquire one by working for it in accordance with his level of development and maturity on the basis of a thought in which the particular idea is contained. The thought is only the shell of the idea which, by means of the mental matrix, reaches the consciousness of the spirit. The idea originates in the causal world.

36. How does the spirit receive thoughts?

The spirit receives all thoughts through the mental matrix, which is a conduit for all thoughts and concepts (imagination).

37. What happens when the mental body transmits thoughts?

When the mental body, or rather the spirit, transmits thoughts, telepathy comes into being, that is the transference of thoughts by means of the Akasha principle without time or space on the mental plane.

38. How is this expressed in the astral and in the material?

These thoughts are received by a very finely developed physical, clairaudient sense of hearing, which passes the thoughts as impressions to the astral clairaudient hearing. From there, the thoughts reach the consciousness of the spirit through the conduit which is the mental matrix, where they become conscious and where they are processed.

39. What is a condensation?

If we accumulate the power of the will, intellect, feelings and manifested belief in an imagined substantial matter, then dynamize and increase the powers by means of opposition or resistance, what comes into being is a condensation of the created matter. That is how we actually make use of the tetrapolar magnet in our consciousness.

40. What is telepathy?

Telepathy is the transmittal of thoughts. As a rule, we transmit thoughts imperatively and also by speaking to a particular person, in order for that person to perform a particular task. We send the thoughts into the mental plane, and the Akasha principle, the Ether, transmits those thoughts without time and space to the spiritual ears of the person for whom they were intended.

41. What is the mental aura?

The mental aura consists of colored radiating attributes of the spirit which are emanated by the tetrapolar magnet or, rather, the mental matrix, with its positive and negative poles.

42. How do timelessness and spacelessness express themselves in the mental kingdom from the human point of view?

From the human point of view, spacelessness and timelessness express themselves in the mental kingdom as an absolute void which is feared by all created things.

43. How do we differentiate between electric and magnetic thoughts from the mental point of view?

On the mental plane, electric thoughts awaken feelings of warmth in us, of being relaxed and at ease; magnetic thoughts give us a feeling of coldness, of constriction.

44. What is mental harmony and what is mental disharmony?

Positive thoughts, imaginations and impressions that we experience on the mental plane awaken feelings of agreement, satisfaction, beauty, joy and sympathy in us. They cause harmony within us.

Negative thoughts, imaginations and impressions awaken dissonance, antipathy, dissatisfaction, ugliness and sadness within us — in other words, disharmony. Both harmony and disharmony are expressions of the absolute lawfulness. We must be able to control both.

45. How do thoughts express themselves positively and negatively and how are they converted?

Active thoughts express themselves positively in the normal consciousness and negative thoughts express themselves in the subconscious. We acquire the ability to differentiate all thoughts, whether positive or negative, through daily introspection in accordance with the four elements and their polarities. We can only conquer negative thoughts by battling with them, namely in four different ways:

1. Through a firm will, i.e. willpower, thereby destroying their effectiveness.
2. Through transmutation, by changing negative thoughts into positive (active) thoughts; in other words, by changing negative thoughts into their opposites, in a passive manner.
3. Through allowing negative thoughts to run through our senses without paying any attention to them until they disappear.
4. Through systematic autosuggestion.

46. Under what circumstances may we employ isolation, transmutation, autosuggestion and the battle?

We use isolation in order not to be infected by the negative attributes or passions of an unbalanced being with which we come into close contact, or in magical operations, for example when we want to make ourselves invisible.

Transmutation not only serves us when converting thoughts and attributes, but also powers, various circum-stances, ailments, moods, sentience, deeds, impressions, perceptions, pictures, and similar things and circumstances, etc., which we change; in all cases *only* noble goals should be pursued.

With autosuggestion, we improve and ennoble our character, our disposition. Furthermore, we strengthen our spirit and prepare him to perform something that we cannot accomplish by means of our normal powers and exercises, and may even achieve success in these cases. This applies only to our astral or psychic and spiritual development.

Through the battle we eliminate negative attributes and overcome any obstacles, especially when it comes to the exercises. We make use of our willpower, the power of the imagination, fixation, our consciousness and other powers and attributes.

47. How do the personal God and the universal God work in the mental sphere?

In the mental realm, the personal God works upon us intuitively and inspirationally. He leads us through thoughts to self-recognition and ennoblement. He guides our divine principle of the eternal spirit so that we get closer to the personal God every day and eventually identify with him.

The universal God in the mental sphere places obstacles in our way up until that point in time when we have all the universal elements and their attributes under our control. This expresses itself especially in introspection, in the exercises, and also in everyday life. The universal God expresses Himself within us in the mental plane as a negative state without time and space, as an absolute nothingness, a void, and also in the conscience.

48. What analogies are there in regards to the mental and the material in comparison to nature? Example: how do alcohol, narcotics and stimulants work?

When consumed on a regular basis, alcohol — especially when it is the object of a passion — dulls our thinking in the mental realm. Therefore it dulls or paralyzes the consciousness and the subconscious, as well as the intellect, memory, speed, perception, the ability to recognize and differentiate, and also the feelings and the will.

Alcohol increases the passion for drunkenness (alcoholism) and, on the material plane, it damages the nervous system to which the cerebrum, the cerebellum and the spinal marrow (cord) belong. Alcohol is a fiery beverage. It contains a strong concentrated dose of the Fire principle. When a person indulges on a consistent basis, it forms a strong disturbance of the Fire element which may intensify until a serious ailment develops which attacks the nervous system and the senses.

The same principle applies when consuming narcotics (drugs) and stimulants. Sometimes it happens that, through over-stimulation, the weakened senses develop a temporary clairvoyance, clairaudience or clairsentience. But these apparent psychic faculties may also be hallucinations. In both instances we are dealing with very harmful manifestations that sometimes lead the individual into mental institutions.

Nature, the lawfulness, reacts to these strongly negative disturbances by returning the situation to balance. A severe trans-dimensional Fire imbalance in both the mental and astral planes often calls forth a state of the fourth dimension, which means that the person perceives himself to be without time or space. At the same time it influences particular senses, especially the eyes, which are controlled by the Fire element. Such a person may suddenly see the surroundings and beings of the otherwise invisible world, or he may experience hallucinations which originate from the influenced subconscious and the over-stimulated senses.

49. The elemental groups in the mental body and the inductive and deductive functions.

In the mental body are the active elemental groups, the elements of Fire and Air. These groups work inductively, rhythmically from the inside to the outside. The negative elemental groups, Water and Earth, work deductively. They constrict, condense and work through the rhythm from the outside to the inside.

50. How are thoughts, maturity, and development registered in the mental sphere, in the causal world, and in the Akasha principle?

In the mental region, thoughts are registered in the cosmic memory, in the causal world as causes, and in the Akasha principle as consequences. Maturity and the state of one's development are registered in the mental region as wisdom.

The level of development of a spirit appears in the causal world as an absolute equilibrium of the elements, whereas in the Akasha principle it appears as a well-balanced human being. Such a well-balanced spirit is no longer subject to destiny but is directly responsible to the Akasha principle or, rather, Providence.

51. What is mental evolution?

Mental evolution is the magical development of the spirit in all his universal elements and their attributes. It leads the spirit to union with God. Basically, it is the step-by-step completion of all divine ideas, beginning with the lowest level and leading up to the highest, which means becoming one with God.

52. What is spiritual yearning?

Spiritual yearning is a longing for self-recognition from a magical and Hermetic point of view, and also becoming aware of the divine principle within oneself. It is also a longing for the recognition of the universal laws in the macro- and microcosm. Yearning is also a particular wish that we send out into the mental plane so that it will be fulfilled. But without the appropriate activity, this wish, this yearning, will not be fulfilled. Should we, however, possess a sincere yearning, but lack the appropriate means or powers to achieve our goal, then the proper path can be pointed out to us in order to reach our goal. In such a case a part of our magical prayer has been fulfilled through our yearning.

53. What does mental polarity mean?
Mental polarity is the active consciousness and the passive subconscious. The electric and magnetic fluids also represent the polarity of the mental region.

54. What are sympathy and antipathy in the mental region?
Sympathy in the mental region denotes that the pleasant thoughts of a particular element fascinate and stimulate us, namely the particular element and the polarity that dominates our character. By way of contrast, thoughts corresponding to other elements awaken aversion and antipathy in us because they belong to an element and a polarity that we cannot tolerate and that disturbs our harmony. Our sympathies and antipathies depend upon the reciprocal effects of the elements.

55. What is considered to be moral harmony in the mental region?
Moral harmony in the mental region is embodied in spiritual asceticism, which means the observance of decency or discipline, purity, and the ordering of our thoughts by having them under control.

56. How can a clairvoyant recognize destiny in the mental region?
He places himself into a state of trance and, by means of the imagination, concentrates into the Akasha principle of the mental region on a particular person. Then he can clearly read the past, present and future of that person. He can achieve the same result by employing a magic mirror.

57. How does mental existence continue in the beyond after the dissolution of the astral body?
After a human being passes over from the material plane, his spirit continues to live in the astral realm with his astral body. Here he loses his astral body on account of the influence of the dissolving elemental processes. Then he automatically passes over into the mental plane, where only his spirit continues to live in the appropriate zone of the mental world. The purer and more balanced the person was on the material plane, the more refined will be the zone he inhabits in the mental world and to which he adapts. Then he returns again to the material world, so that he completely balances, ennobles and perfects himself.

58. The psychic states: trance mediumship, clairvoyance and spiritualism.

When an individual transposes himself with his consciousness into the solar plexus of his body and connects with the Akasha principle, the so-called state of trance comes into being. True mediumship is the passive contact with an invisible being. This mediumship is under the control of our will, which also governs the contact.

Clairvoyance is the ability of a human being to clearly see whatever he wishes to see, whether the physical eyes are open or closed, whether in the visible or the invisible world. It does not matter if a crystal or glass ball, a magic mirror or the polished surface of a wardrobe, cupboard etc. is used. The quality of the things seen depends upon the magician's purity of character. Clairvoyance depends upon:

1. Aptitude, talent,
2. The maturity of the magician, and
3. Astral development.

These abilities are developed primarily through the universal light.

Spiritualism is a passive and uncontrolled contact with the beings of the invisible world through a medium who has transposed himself into a state of trance through prayer, ecstasy or other means. This procedure is very harmful. Although the medium may sometimes contact a particularly good astral being, they usually mistake phantoms for the spirits of the departed. Through the repetition of particular thoughts, one may create hundreds of such phantoms; sometimes the subconscious of a particular medium is also involved in their creation.

A spiritualistic medium, or rather a human being, is merely an instrument of uncontrollable powers who subjects himself without his own will to the harmful influences of lower astral beings.

59. What does the term "moonstruck" (somnambulism) mean?

To be "moonstruck" is to suffer from an ailment of the soul that comes into being through a serious disturbance of the electromagnetic fluid. Those who suffer from this ailment have an extremely disturbed magnetic fluid, through which the gravitation of that particular person wanes, that is, he loses contact with the gravitational force of the earth. This condition generally occurs during the night while the person is asleep, and is caused by the influence of the moon. The person who is "struck" by it becomes as light as a feather, can move like a fly on the wall and can also scale the most dangerous and highest places without any effort. He can even walk on telephone wires. This is a pathological manifestation.

60. What are possession, epilepsy, and St. Vitus' Dance, and what are the causes of these ailments?

Possession or obsession originates with hallucinations. We are dealing here with a particular splitting of the consciousness (schizophrenia) wherein various impressions influence us by means of our five senses unexpectedly, undesirably and without anyone's help. It is a pathological, undesirable state.

Epilepsy and St. Vitus' Dance are ailments that come into being due to a polarity disturbance that results from a disturbed equilibrium between the mental and astral planes. These ailments are healed through the polarity. For example, the brain of a woman is electric; therefore it can be healed with magnetism. A man's brain is magnetic; therefore it can be healed with electricity.

61. Mental stimulation: for example incense, religious music, and prayer.

To better perform magical operations or to come into contact with spiritual beings in the invisible world, we use stimulants to enter the fourth dimension by influencing our senses in the mental region through incense, religious music and prayer.

62. The language of communication on the mental plane. How does one spirit speak to another?

On the mental plane, one spirit generally communicates with another pictorially, through gestures and symbols similar to those which the subconscious shows us when we are asleep. The more advanced spirits communicate among each other through clairaudience, by way of which they understand all languages.

63. How are perceptions transmitted?

Perceptions are transmitted through our physical and astral senses and then through the mental matrix to the consciousness of the spirit, who processes them by means of the astral and material bodies.

64. What is mental passivity?

Mental passivity is produced when a person passively subjects his will — or, rather, the negative attributes in his subconscious — to another. Such a person puts himself in a dependent position.

Mental passivity may also be defined as an absolute indifference towards one's negative attributes during introspection. That, of course, occurs while a person is under the control of his own will.

65. What is a natural mental state?
It is the state of the spirit in the Akasha principle, without thoughts, sentience, or perceptions, and without time and space or activity of the spirit; it is absolute rest, nothingness, void.

Questions Concerning The Astral Plane

1. What does the word "astral" indicate?
The astral world and the astral body of a human being exist through the Akasha principle, from which they have originated through the labor of the electric and magnetic fluids. The astral plane exists in space, where we find everything that has taken place on earth so far — what is occurring now and what will happen later, in other words the past, present and future.

There are vibrations of the electric and magnetic fluids in the Ether or Akasha principle out of which everything was created. In the astral plane we find the foundation of life, of all existence: light, darkness, sound, color and rhythm. All these things have their origin there. The astral plane is the emanation of the eternal, the fourth dimension. In the astral plane live the souls of the departed, the elementaries, the larvae, the beings of the pure elements, water sprites, wood fairies, satyrs etc.

The beings that belong to the pure elements are the salamanders of the Fire element, the sylphs of the Air element, the undines or mermaids of the Water element, and the gnomes of the Earth element. In accordance with its figurative significance, the astral can also be the highest Akasha principle which created the astral world and which also controls it.

2. What kind of fundamental attributes does the astral body contain?
The fundamental attributes of the astral body, in accordance with the elements, are endurance (Fire), diligence (Air), patience (Water), and systematics (Earth).

3. How does the astral body sustain its life and what is its nourishment?
The astral body sustains its life through the presence of the eternal spirit and it nourishes itself through breathing.

4. What functions do the elements have in the astral body?
The functions of the elements in the astral body are identical with the functions of the elements in the material body. The Fire element in its positive (active) polarity represents the constructive function, whereas in its negative polarity it is the destructive function; in other words it destroys everything. The element of Water enlivens everything in the active pole, while in the opposite pole it dissolves and destroys every-

thing. Air is the equilibrating or compensating principle between Fire and Water. The Earth element connects all the elements and keeps them together through reinforcement and solidification; it is the cause of the growth and death of the astral body.

5. *How does a characteristic express itself in the astral body?*
Depending upon which element predominates in the astral body of a human being, we differentiate four temperaments or characteristics:

1. The choleric temperament is analogous to the Fire element.
2. The sanguine temperament is analogous to the Air element.
3. The melancholic temperament is analogous to the Water element.
4. The phlegmatic temperament is analogous to the Earth element.

In accordance with the intensity (dynamic) of the polarity of the individual elements, we are dealing either with a more or less balanced character.

6. *What is the astral aura?*
The astral aura is made up of the emanating elemental effects[2] of the various colored attributes that emanate from the positive and negative poles of the tetrapolar astral magnet.

7. *What holds the mental and astral bodies together?*
The mental body is linked to the astral body by the mental matrix on account of the electromagnetic influences of the elements.

8. *Is the astral body mortal?*
The astral body is mortal; it is merely an instrument of the eternal spirit.

9. *What happens on the other side when the mental body leaves the astral body?*
When the spirit leaves the astral body on the astral plane, the astral body dissolves back into the original substances from which it was created.

10. *What functions does the astral body perform while asleep?*
Since the astral body possesses the same functions as the physical body, it rests during sleep and more effectively inhales the astral substances through which it

---

[2] In this case, the term "elemental effects" refers to the effects of the elements. This usage applies throughout this book whenever the verb "elemental" is used in front of a noun, and should not be confused with the being that is called an "elemental." – ED.

thoroughly strengthens itself. Besides that, with its senses it serves as an instrument for the expressions of the subconscious, whose activity is highest during sleep.

11. Occult capabilities of the astral body.

The astral body can have the following occult capabilities: clairvoyance, clairaudience, and clairsentience, also paranormal taste and smell. All of these together represent the absolute elemental equilibrium. The astral body and the spirit can loosen themselves from the physical body through the loosening of the elemental life-cord (exteriorization) which connects the astral and physical bodies. With the spirit, the astral body can pass over into the astral plane (astral travel). The astral body can make herself invisible and can separate independently from the spiritual and material bodies.

Through psychometry, a magician can achieve an astral connection with any person who has come into contact with a particular object through which the magician can read the events that concern the past, present and future of the object.

The astral body can become a medium under the control of the will; it can connect and identify with every intelligence, with every higher divine being and with every divinity. The soul, or, rather, the astral body, is capable, after an appropriate preliminary phase of development, of gathering and controlling all elements within herself and working with them internally and externally. The astral body is an instrument with which to control the Akasha principle; by means of the Akasha principle, it can consciously transpose itself into a state of trance. The astral body also serves the purpose of utilizing the elements from the Akasha with the help of individual rituals. The soul can be impregnated with the four highest divine attributes (virtues).

12. The electric and magnetic capabilities of the astral body.

We can fill or impregnate the astral body with warmth, light and the electric fluid; on the other hand we can condense in the astral body with coolness and constriction. The astral matrix possesses both electric and magnetic attributes. Clairvoyance is an electric ability of the astral body; clairsentience and psychometry are magnetic abilities. We may place mediumship into the proper order of the sphere of the magnetic fluid. In accordance with the polarity of the tetrapolar magnet, the choleric (Fire), sanguine (Air), melancholic (Water) or phlegmatic (Earth) temperaments can express themselves in the soul.

The aura, which emanates colored attributes, can be either electric or magnetic in accordance with the temperament. In the soul exist elemental centers; the spirit makes use of the powers that are in these centers for particular tasks. The *svadhisthana chakra* is the center of the Water element, and has magnetic capabilities and powers. The *manipura chakra* is the center of the Fire element and possesses electric powers and capabilities. The central channel or *sushumna* connects the highest elemental center, the *sahasrara chakra*, with the other elemental centers (lotuses) through which the Akasha principle, with the so-called *ida* (the electric fluid) and *pingala* (the magnetic fluid), passes.

13. How does the polarity in the astral body express itself?
The polarity in the astral body expresses itself through the radiating poles of the tetrapolar magnet. The result is the colored, emanating aura. A clairvoyant can recognize the basic characteristics of a person's character and its individual attributes through the colors in the aura.

14. What are harmony and disharmony in the astral body?
Harmony in the astral body corresponds with the elemental equilibrium and the consonance or unison of the electric and magnetic fluids in the tetrapolar magnet. Disharmony is an imbalance of the elemental attributes and corresponds with the activity of the electric and magnetic fluids. Both harmony and disharmony are, of course, expressions of the lawfulness.

15. By what means is the astral body influenced?
The astral body is influenced primarily through introspection, astral asceticism, active powers and attributes of the positive and negative kind, various exercises, prayers, autosuggestion, suggestion, realization of divine ideas and becoming aware of one's own "I." In short, it can be said that we influence the astral body principally through ennoblement and perfection in every direction and through the development of all aspects of our character.

16. What is meant by the vitality of the astral body?
The vitality of the astral body is the vital energy which, in the Akasha principle or *sushumna*, streams forth as the electromagnetic fluid, the *ida* and *pingala* which flow out from the highest elemental center, the *sahasrara* (thousand-petaled lotus). This vital energy supplies and connects all the elemental centers in the soul.

17. How does mental influence upon the astral body express itself?
Mental influence upon the astral body expresses itself with the help of the mental matrix, which directs and maintains the activity of the spirit on the astral plane.

18. What is the so-called astral filter?
The astral filter is the conscience, the Akasha principle, through which every thought, perception, circumstance and impression passes.

19. Fluid condensers and their effect in the astral body.

We understand the term "fluid condensers" to mean the accumulators in which, for an unlimited time, the powers of the electric and magnetic fluids or the energies of the universal elements gather and maintain themselves. Should the occasion arise, they are charged with an appropriate wish or task through the help of the Akasha principle. The condensers are prepared from solid, liquid and airy (because of the fragrances) substances that possess an excess of accumulatory abilities. Fluid condensers serve the influence by means of the elements or the development of the astral senses.

For normal use, simple fluid condensers suffice. But in order to accumulate especially powerful amounts of energy, or when working on matters which are intended to produce a physical influence with the help of mental or astral influences (for example when creating elementaries or wax dolls, bringing pictures to life and other materialization manifestations), we will of course require complex fluid condensers from plant extracts.

20. How are disturbances in the astral body expressed?

Disturbances in the astral body express themselves in the form of various astral ailments, for example: astral retardation, somnambulism, epilepsy, unbalanced negative attributes, feeble-mindedness and other astral ailments (ailments of the soul). These ailments are caused by severe disturbances of the electric and magnetic fluids; therefore they also cause disturbances between the astral and physical bodies, or between the astral and mental bodies.

21. Astral healing methods.

We heal astral ailments through intensely concentrated vital energy which we impregnate with the wish for the patient's complete recovery. We draw this accumulated vital energy directly from the universe and direct it into the astral body of the ailing person without passing it through our own body. Through this we prevent the weakening of our own vitality and at the same time prevent the mixing of our Od (character) with the Od of the ailing person; otherwise we can infect ourselves with the negative attributes of the patient.

Some ailments, such as somnambulism, epilepsy and St. Vitus' Dance, can be healed by strengthening the fluid which is lacking. Wherever a disturbance between the mental and astral bodies exists, a magician can undertake the removal of such a disturbance through the appropriate reinforcement or weakening of the elements, or of the electric or magnetic fluids.

22. What is exteriorization?

Exteriorization is a conscious separation of the astral body from the physical body. First, with our mental body, we step out of the material body; then, with the help of the imagination and the will, we draw the astral body out of the physical body. Following that, we step again with our mental body into the astral body and begin to breathe in the astral body. From that moment on, the physical body ceases to breathe.

The physical body is connected to the astral and mental bodies with a silvery shining life-cord (astral matrix). If, during exteriorization, someone were to touch the seemingly dead physical body, the life-cord would immediately tear and a real physical death would result.

23. What is a perfect astral body?
A perfect astral body has become completely one with God.

24. What function do the astral and mental bodies have in view of the physical body?
The astral body is the center of all attributes and powers of the spirit. It is the instrument of the eternal spirit in the astral plane and, through its senses, it receives all the perceptions of the physical world. These perceptions are transferred onto the mental matrix, which in turn directs all thoughts and perceptions to the consciousness of the spirit. The spirit processes (connects) thoughts and perceptions by means of the astral and physical bodies.

The astral body transfers its functions through the electromagnetic influence of the tetrapolar magnet to the physical body, which realizes them on the physical plane. All these functions are, of course, guided by the eternal spirit. The astral body is connected to the mental body by the mental matrix and to the physical body by the astral matrix.

25. How does the Akasha affect the astral body?
The Akasha affects the astral body through the power of the active will of the eternal spirit — who is a part of the Akasha principle — through the power of the imagination and through manifested belief, consequently through creative power. The Akasha principle is effective through the electro-magnetic fluid of the mental matrix (which represents the finest spiritual substance in a human being) and directs everything to the astral body onto its astral matrix. In other words, the tetrapolar magnet emanates the attributes and energies of the eternal spirit in the polarity of the astral matrix. In this manner the eternal spirit directs all the functions of the elements in the astral body.

26. What is the karma of the astral body?
The karma of the astral body consists of all the causes which a human being has created for himself in the astral plane. These causes, be they positive or negative, cause effects and consequences in the astral plane. All of this is also meticulously registered or recorded in the causal world of the astral plane.

27. *How can the lifespan of the astral body be prolonged and what is its specific influence upon the spiritual substance?*

The life span of the astral body may be prolonged by a continuous ennoblement of the human character, with all its attributes, until absolute elemental equilibrium has been achieved. We ennoble ourselves in this manner, and at the same time we also ennoble the mental and physical bodies through which this elemental equilibrium automatically passes over to the mental and astral matrices. When this occurs, the physical, astral and mental bodies achieve complete health and their life is prolonged.

28. *The astral kingdom and its analogous relationship to the astral body.*

The astral world, also known as the astral plane, is an invisible world, created from the Akasha principle by means of the electric and magnetic fluids of the tetrapolar magnet.

At times the astral plane is also called the fourth dimension (without time and space) because everything which has occurred, is occurring or will occur in the material world — in other words the past, present and future — is hidden there. In this plane, electric and magnetic vibrations move and spread. Everything created has its origin here: light, darkness, sound, color, rhythm — the entire spectrum of life.

The astral world exists in space. That is where the souls of departed human beings live, as well as the elementaries, larvae, and the beings of the four pure elements: salamanders in the Fire element, sylphs in the Air element, undines or mermaids in the Water element, gnomes in the Earth element. Furthermore there are satyrs, sylvas, water sprites etc.

The astral body consists of the same substance as the astral plane; it is therefore analogous to it. The astral body nourishes itself from this substance; it inhales it. All the functions of the elements, of movement, of the tree of life, are also analogous to the astral world. The beings that live in the astral world have a transitory life, just like the astral body of a human being.

29. *What is the genius of the astral body?*

The genius of the astral body is awakened through the impregnation of the astral body with the highest divine virtues that correspond to the four universal elements.

30. *What are mediumship and spiritualism?*

Mediumship is an attribute that allows the astral, physical and spiritual bodies to be influenced in a passive manner by particular beings and powers. This mediality can also be present consciously under our will and our control as well as during passive contact with invisible beings or powers; without the participation of the will, it becomes an uncontrolled mediation with uncontrolled beings and powers of the invisible world, which is called spiritualism.

31. Preparation of the astral body with divine attributes.
The preparation of the astral body with divine attributes refers to the achievement of omnipotence: wisdom and omniscience, all-encompassing love or mercy and immortality. These four fundamental attributes of the universal elements distinguish themselves through omnipresence. This is the concrete connection, and eventually the identification, with the highest divine idea in the astral body.

32. The occult significance of morals regarding the astral body.
We consider the astral body to be the purest and most beautiful astral instrument of the eternal spirit, who is the center of the absolutely pure positive and negative attributes and whom we continuously ennoble. This is the origin of the phrase: "I am that I am!" (Exodus 3:14)

33. What is sleep?
Sleep is an unconscious state during which the physical and astral bodies are at rest. Only the subconscious in the spirit works without time and space. The impressions with which the mental body nourishes and satisfies itself during the day are sorted during sleep. In other words, they are brought into the proper relationship with the thoughts of the subconscious. During sleep the mental body is charged and strengthened with new energy, endowing us with the familiar feeling of being "newly refreshed." If necessary, advice is also given through dreams, which usually refers to the general structure or planning of one's life.

34. What is a dream?
A dream is an expression of our subconscious, which continues to work during sleep, when our normal consciousness is dormant and at rest. As a rule, dreams are distorted reflective events that always concern our attributes, capabilities and spirit. Sometimes dreams teach or warn us through symbols. They speak to us in the language of nature, in pictures.

35. How does the subconscious work in the astral body?
The subconscious works in the astral body through negative attributes, such as passions, indecencies, and thoughts, imaginations and pictures — which, of course, are not sufficiently condensed to manifest on the physical plane. However, the subconscious can express itself in a situation (opportunity, temptation) which fulfills certain favorable conditions in order to manifest on the material plane.

36. How do negative attributes manifest themselves from the astral into the mental and physical bodies?

Perceptions filled with thoughts and pictures as expressions of negative or positive attributes are perceived and received through our physical, mental and astral senses. By means of the mental matrix, perceptions penetrate to the subconscious of the spirit, which seeks to realize them — without our will but with the help of the astral, mental or physical bodies, depending upon which plane the subconscious of the spirit has chosen for their realization. This is practically and automatically carried out by the universal elements of the tetrapolar magnet in accordance with their functions. The guiding force is the subconscious.

37. How are positive and negative situations from the mental plane or mental body created across the astral world into the physical body and the material world?

1. First of all, a particular thought appears in our intellect in the mental plane and, if applicable, with a picture, an imagination. This process falls into the activity sphere of the Air element. At the same time, the thought receives a coloration in accordance with the feeling, that is, an activity of the Water element. And since we are dealing with the expression of an active attribute, our will and our belief develops the concept through the imagination and passes it on to the consciousness by means of the mental matrix.

Through the intensive effectiveness of the conscious-ness, the attribute, thought or picture reaches the astral plane via the astral matrix. On the astral plane, a concentration takes place under the influence of the electric and magnetic fluids through the power of constriction — through neutralization of the Air element and solidification of the Earth element. This all happens through the activity of the spirit in the astral body, in the astral plane, already in space.

Now we have reached the point where the powers of the elements that have formed this situation begin to condense and fortify themselves intensely. When this happens, the situation becomes a reality on the physical plane through the effectiveness of the elements, which possess the same functions as the elements in the astral plane.

The effectiveness in the physical plane becomes reality in space and time from the causal world to the material plane.

Should the spirit decide that an attribute or concept, a thought or picture should become a reality in the mental body, on the mental plane, then the original state is maintained without change, or in other words, without time or space in the mental plane or the causal plane.

2. When creating a situation on the astral plane in the passive sense, we use the same procedure as in the active sense. But instead of working with the will, belief or

imagination, and normal consciousness, our subconscious works with its passive attributes in suitable surroundings and with favorable conditions. It is of course very important for us to distinguish the positive from the negative and to battle against the negative. We should never allow negativity to become predominant in us.

38. What kind of influence can entities exert upon the astral body?
Entities or beings from the invisible world cannot influence the magician's astral body when he consciously contacts such entities — provided, of course that he has the beings and their effective powers under his will and his control, and that he uses this connection only for noble purposes. Should these beings be higher intelligences or guardian spirits, they can influence his astral body under his will, if he so wishes, in accordance with his level of development. They can strengthen his active attributes and powers and also his health, and fulfill his various wishes in a positive, good sense.

In the case of spiritualistic mediums, various lower and higher beings — for example, the souls of departed human beings, their shadows, phantoms or larvae — can generally influence the astral bodies of these mediums, either in a positive or a negative sense.

39. What are the chakras in the astral body?
According to Hindu philosophy, these are the elemental centers in the astral body which are directed through the highest elemental center, the *sahasrara* or thousand-petaled lotus, and which are connected with each other through the so-called *sushumna* or Akasha principle.

40. What are the ida, pingala and sushumna in the astral body and what is their function from the astral point of view?
Ida is an electric fluid and *pingala* a magnetic fluid. Both flow through the *sushumna* by means of the Akasha principle. The *sushumna* extends from the highest elemental center, the *sahasrara* (which is under the crown of the head) all the way down the spinal cord to connect all the other elemental centers, all the way to the *muladhara chakra*. The *ida* and *pingala* actually correspond to the tetrapolar magnet with its dual polarity. They strengthen the elemental centers in the astral body and, together with the Akasha, they form the quintessence of our vital energy.

41. How do the four divine attributes express themselves in the astral body in an average person and in a perfected human being?
The average human being imagines the four highest divine attributes to exist outside of his person. In accordance with his religious concepts, there is an almighty, wise, omniscient, loving, merciful and immortal God in heaven. In the astral body these

divine attributes express themselves clearly in his belief, as intellect, love, devotion and consciousness.

A perfected human being has unified the aforementioned four highest divine attributes through identification with God within himself, realized through a step-by-step process of development, which means that he has impregnated his astral body with the highest divine attributes. He eventually joins these divine attributes into one idea, and this enables him to experience and manifest the concept of God in the astral body in the highest possible form.

42. The problematic nature of clairvoyance and clairaudience. Their development and eventual pathological consequences.

Clairvoyance and *clairaudience* are occult abilities of seeing and hearing outside of time and space. It does not matter whether we are dealing with clairvoyance or clairaudience in the past, present or future, or seeing and hearing departed human beings, or other similar cases. There are different kinds of *clairvoyance*:

1. The best kind of clairvoyance occurs when you are born with the ability.

2. Clairvoyance may be caused through the involuntary displacement of the elements in the spirit in the mental body or through severe shocks or impacts to the brain on account of various ailments. Especially as the result of a stroke or in cases of emotional ailments, people may sometimes develop clairvoyant abilities to a greater or lesser degree. Mediumistic people who can bring about clairvoyance through invisible beings belong to this group. People who forcibly induce clairvoyance by means of narcotics such as opium, hashish etc., also belong to this group. All the cases that belong to this second group are harmful to human health on all planes; many who are afflicted with the above conditions eventually end up in mental institutions. No one who wishes to attain clairvoyance should ever use such questionable and harmful means.

3. Another method through which clairvoyance can be attained is through the weakening or temporary paralysis of the organ of sight. Fixing upon an object in the magic mirror, gazing at a crystal ball or precious stone may also bring about clairvoyance, but these methods are not suitable for everyone. When employing such methods, the optic nerve should not be influenced; instead, the above-mentioned objects should merely serve as aids for the eyes of a magician who is already clairvoyant. Clairvoyance rests upon talent or astral development, and is solely dependent upon the maturity of the magician.

4. Ultimately we should favor the kind of clairvoyance that we acquire through appropriate magical development, namely exercises for the eyes. For this kind of development we need a clear concept of the universal light as an aspect of Fire, which, by way of magical correspondence, belongs to the eye and the will. We will not achieve the proper success without a distinct, natural and visible concept of the universal light. We take in the universal light, first by inhaling it into our entire physical body and astral body, then by transposing it into both physical eyes, then into the astral eyes, and then condensing it in the eyeballs. Into this light we focus or concentrate the attribute of clairvoyance by imagining that the universal light penetrates everything, sees everything clearly, and that time and space are no obstacle for the universal light. We retain this light in the eyes for about ten minutes and then allow it to disperse back into the universe, so that our eyes return to their normal state. Otherwise we will not be able to distinguish between the perceptions of our normal eyesight or our clairvoyant eyes. In order to achieve clairvoyance more quickly, we can use a magical water, one of the so-called fluid condensers.

Clairaudience: The development of clairaudience is the same as for clairvoyance. Through clairaudience, we can perceive voices over vast distances. Clairaudience may also express itself within us as thinking out loud, coming from our innermost, either from the area of the heart or the solar plexus. After thorough schooling, we can comprehend everything through clairaudience just as if we were speaking to someone normally. Everything that has been said about clairvoyance in regards to the circumstances which bring about pathological problems applies to clairaudience and clairsentience as well. For the development of clairaudience we can use a strong decoction of chamomile and distilled water as a fluid condenser. We then moisten two cotton swabs with the fluid condenser and fill them with the condensed Air element (which we have impregnated with the concept that is to bring about clairaudience). We then place the cotton swabs that have been prepared in this manner half-way into our auditory canal. We introduce the Akasha principle into our entire head, transfer our consciousness into both ears, and imagine the ability of absolute clairaudience. After a prolonged period of meditation and concentration we dissolve the Akasha principle into the universal Akasha, remove the cotton swabs from our ears, and store them in a safe place so that they do not fall into the wrong hands.

Questions Concerning The Physical Plane

1. *The physical body and its anatomy.*

The physical body came into being from the Akasha principle through the effects of the electric and magnetic fluids. Everything that happens and exists in the universe or macrocosm also happens and exists in the human body or microcosm. That is why Divine Providence faithfully reflects itself in human beings. Health is a very important factor in the human body. From the Hermetic point of view, health is a complete harmony of all the powers that are active in the human body in respect to the fundamental attributes of the elements. In order to attain perfect health we have to maintain the elemental equilibrium in our body.

The human body is nourished and maintained through eating and breathing, which produce the combustion process in the body. Therefore, our life depends upon the intake of nourishment and breathing. However, our nourishment contains the elemental substances in irregular proportions. Therefore we have to eat various kinds of food, so that all the elements obtain their required amount of fuel. If we supply our body with only one kind of nourishment, it will become sick, because a particular element will have failed to receive the necessary nourishment.

In the human body the elements are distributed in the following manner: The Fire element in the head, the Air element in the chest, the Water element in the abdominal area, and the Earth element throughout the entire body, in the flesh, muscles and bones. The purposes or functions of the elements are constructive, equilibrating and destructive. In its positive polarity, the Fire element works in an invigorating and constructive way, whereas it works destructively in its negative polarity. The Water element works in a constructive and maintaining way in its positive polarity, but in its negative state it decomposes and destroys everything. The Air element is neutral; it equilibrates the effects of the Water and Fire elements through breathing. In the positive sense it is invigorating and in the negative sense destructive. Earth holds all the elements together through its condensation, firmness and reinforcement (solidification). In the positive sense it supports growth, the maturity of the body, and in the negative sense it causes aging, weakness and death. The Earth element works in the human body as a tetrapolar magnet, as the electromagnetic fluid, in which other elements become particularly effective.

In addition to their principal seats in the human body, the elements work specifically in accordance with their polarities in every organ or part of the body. In particular organs, the electrical fluid is effective from the inside to the outside and the magnetic fluid from the outside to the inside, whereas when it comes to other organs the opposite is the case. The reason for this is that the course and function of the elements is harmoniously and analogously balanced in the entire organism. In the Hermetic sciences, the knowledge of the polarities of the electric and magnetic fluids is called the occult anatomy of the body.

2. How is the physical body kept alive?
The human body is kept alive through the intake of nourishment and through breathing, the so-called combustion process.

3. How are the material, astral and mental bodies kept together?
The material and astral bodies are kept together by the astral matrix. The astral and mental bodies are kept together by the mental matrix. In both cases this occurs under the influence of the elemental effects, through the so-called labor of the elements.

4. The effectiveness of the elements in the body.
The universal elements of Fire, Air, Water, Earth and Akasha are effective in the body. The element of Fire is in the head — everything active takes place there. The Air element is predominant in the chest area, which, through breathing, automatically equilibrates the effects of Fire and Water. The Water element is effective in the abdominal area by chemically processing liquid substances and through elimination. The aforementioned elements are kept together by the Earth element in the legs and in the entire body, but mainly in the flesh, muscles and bones. Earth limits the other elements in their activities through its firmness and constriction. The Earth element causes the growth, maturity and aging of the human organism. The Akasha principle expresses itself in vitality, which means in the reciprocal effects of blood and sperm.

5. The electric and magnetic influence and their causes.
If we are under the influence of the electric fluid, then the Fire element is more effective in us. In this case we feel hot, or we are active to higher degrees, we work more diligently, and therefore we are internally satiated with the Fire element.

Through the increased influence of the magnetic fluids we perceive coldness; should the magnetic fluid becomes satiated within us, elimination increases.

6. What differences exist between the electric and magnetic influences and their effectiveness?
The electric influence expresses itself within us in the choleric temperament and in the will. The magnetic influence expresses itself in the melancholic temperament and in belief. On the surface of the human body, the electromagnetic fluid is effective as radiating life-magnetism. The right side of the body is (in the case of a right-handed person) the active or electrical side, whereas the left side of the body is passive or magnetic. The opposite is the case with a left-handed person.

The electric fluid, through its expansion, causes radiating electrons on the inside of every body, which on the other hand are attracted by the magnetic fluid of the earth. The electric fluid is located in the Inner of everything created, therefore also in the center of the earth, while the magnetic fluid is effective on the surface of the earth and on everything created. The activities of the electric fluid express themselves through warmth and expansion, while the magnetic fluid expresses itself through coolness and constriction. The differences between the effects of the electric and magnetic fluids cause the attractive force (gravitational pull) of the earth or the weight or gravity of the earth. The electric fluid produces the acids in all organic or inorganic bodies or substances from a chemical or alchemical point of view, whereas the magnetic fluid is effective in an alkaline manner.

7. *How can the material body be influenced from the Hermetic point of view (Eucharist)?*

The physical body can be influenced through air, water and food, provided we place particular wishes for the ennoblement of our body into that air, water and food in order to reach the highest goal, to gain the elemental equilibrium and similar objectives, as for example: health, energy, success, rest etc. The Akasha principle transfers these wishes to the impregnated substances we take into our body and blood in the form of breathing, water (beverages), or any other nourishment for the material body. But from here, the wishes are transmitted through the electromagnetic fluid via the astral and mental matrices to the consciousness of the spirit, the highest Akasha organ, which realizes our wishes.

8. *How does the polarity express itself in men and women?*

The polarity expresses itself in men through creative power and in women through the ability to bear children. This also applies to sexual intercourse. In the case of a man, the positive creative power is contained in the sexual organs, as is the passive or bearing power in the case of a woman. For particular magical operations the female magician or female partner must be schooled in the control of the electric and magnetic fluids and must change the polarities within herself so that, during sexual intercourse, her head becomes the embodiment of the magnetic fluid and her sexual organs the electric fluid. In this case the man's polarity remains unchanged; the head must possess the magnetic polarity and the sexual organs the electric polarity.

9. *Sexual magic.*

The magico-sexual operation, in which we place the purest, noblest wishes and tasks, is a sacred act, a prayer through which we emulate the act of cosmic love, because everything that was created in the cosmos has become a reality through the act of love. Sexual magic is based on this universal law.

During this union, an excessive dual polar tension of the energies — which releases an enormous effect — comes into being between the two partners. Rather than a new life, it is a correspondent cause and effect which is created during this act of love. The tetrapolar magnet Yod-Heh-Vau-Heh functions as a volt during this sacred act, and this belongs to the highest mystery of love in creation.

10. *The fundamental laws of the physical materia.*
The fundamental laws of the physical materia are time, space, weight and measure as the effects of the creative activities of the tetrapolar magnet.

11. *What are ailments of the body from the Hermetic point of view, and how can they be influenced?*
Ailments of the human body come into being through a severe disturbance of the elemental functions of the electric and magnetic fluids or through disharmony between the physical, astral and mental bodies. Ailments may also be the result of karma. They can be influenced by substances with opposite effects, as in allopathic medicine, or with substances of the same foundation as the ailment itself, as in homeopathy. Besides natural healing, healing can be achieved through the effects of the elements, through the electric and magnetic fluids of the healer or Magnetopath, provided that he has these fluids in excess. Ailments can also be healed and influenced with various other methods: for example, by means of beings from the invisible world, mummial magic, the negative state, asceticism, vampirism, abstract imagination, sexual magic, electrical current and magnetism, *prana* (vital energy), prayer, ritual, sympathetic magic, Kabbalistic formulae or with the help of genii.

12. *From the Hermetic point of view, what is blood and what is sperm?*
Blood and sperm are carriers of the Akasha principle. The reciprocal effects of these two substances express themselves in vitality.

13. *How are physical deeds registered in the Akasha?*
Physical deeds are registered simultaneously as causes and effects in the causal world and on the physical plane.

14. *How can the past, present and future be read?*
A magician can read or see the past, present and future by means of a magic mirror. He places himself into a state of trance and, through his imagination, focuses on the pictures. In this manner he can read in the Akasha the past, present and future of anyone.

15. How is a body prepared for a particular purpose, such as healing? (Concerning materialization)

For the purpose of healing, either the entire body or just the hands can be impregnated with vital energy which can then be transferred to the ailing person, the afflicted organ or the ailing part of the body.

For materialization, a magician can condense a particular element, whether within or outside of himself, to such a degree that, when projecting it into a particular matter or concept, the matter or concept materializes and can be touched and seen even by those who are not schooled in magic.

16. Preparation of the body for astral contact.

To prepare our body for the astral plane it must be filled with astral substance, in other words with that part of the Akasha principle that contains the electricity and magnetism of the astral light in space.

17. How can the body be rejuvenated? Various methods, laws and conditions.

The physical body can be rejuvenated through life elixirs. Essences are used for the mental plane, tinctures for the astral plane, and salts or extracts for the physical plane. According to the alchemists, the philosophers' stone, the red tincture or green lion, is a concentrated energy from all four elements as well as the fifth, which is a quintessence. A larger amount not only heals any ailment and increases vitality, but also rejuvenates the entire body.

Astral elixirs are alchemical accumulators. They serve the purpose of reaching a sufficient elemental equilibrium, so that from this we can make use of every element. In the state of rejuvenation, it is the electrical Fire element that serves astral rejuvenation. That is why rejuvenation in the astral manner is the most effective method and is without any danger.

An alchemist or Hermetic who controls the elements can concentrate these rejuvenating elemental attributes into physical elixirs and essences. Through this procedure, elixirs become magically effective when charged with the appropriate element (fluidified), and their effect extends upon the substance and the astral of the one who uses them.

The mental elixir represents an ideational, intellectual, imaginary concept of absolute recovery, rejuvenation and conservation, and through this we experience our thoughts through feelings. We can condense these thoughts or cover them with astral fluid and, at the same time, we can produce the precondition for success, rejuvenation and similar attributes for physical purposes.

A Hermetic who wants to enjoy the elixir of life fully must be familiar with all the analogies of the physical, astral and mental. He must know their elemental effects and must have these elements completely under his control. The preparation of an elixir is simply an application of the elemental procedure of nature. We can also call forth the process of rejuvenation of the physical and astral bodies through autosuggestion.

Rejuvenation of the physical and astral bodies has, of course, its shadowy side. In accordance with the universal law of development of human beings, we return to our younger years during rejuvenation, and — because we not only rejuvenate our physical bodies but our astral and mental bodies as well — we lose our experiences and knowledge, including the wisdom and experiences of our Hermetic work of years past, depending on how many years younger we have become. Any good magician must consider whether or not he wants to pay such a high spiritual and astral price for just a few years of youth.

18. *The effect of stimulants upon the material and mental bodies.*

Stimulants dull the thinking and call forth undesirable apparitions as a consequence of disturbances between the electric and magnetic fluids, especially in the mental region. Sometimes this may cause the derailing of particular sensory organs, for example when sight, hearing and feeling slip into the fourth dimension. It all depends on what the person is trying to achieve by using these stimulants. Through such methods, a person may, for a short time, become clairvoyant, clairaudient or clairsentient.

As a rule, lower astral beings like to exploit such opportunities. They often proclaim themselves in this manner through a medium who functions without the control of his own will. A state produced through stimulants is always harmful, especially when uncontrolled, because it has been produced suddenly and with force, in an unnatural manner. At the same time the mental senses (thinking, the Air element and its aspects) are very severely affected by this.

The nerves in the physical body are dulled through this harmful intervention; the heart is weakened and the sensory organs are harmed. All of this also has a very harmful influence upon the astral body, the senses, and upon the electric and magnetic fluids, whose functions can be dangerously disturbed. Should an experiment with stimulants for some reason be repeated frequently (for example, because of a passion or yearning for an intoxicated state or to achieve clairvoyance, clairaudience and clairsentience), the physical body becomes strongly accustomed to these stimulants to the point that the person no longer has any defenses. Such a person wastes away.

The physical, astral and spiritual bodies, the senses and the intellect become dulled until the condition turns into a recognizable astral and physical ailment.

19. *Harmony and disharmony in the body and their causes.*

Harmony is a common labor which is in unison with all the elements that are effective in the human body. Harmony expresses itself in the complete health of the soul and spirit, in the development of the body, in beauty and in vigor.

Disharmony expresses itself in the human body through disturbances of the functions of the elements. If an ailment is already present, then we are dealing with the severe, serious and visible disturbance of an element. Harmony and disharmony are expressions of lawfulness.

20. What is youth and what is aging?

Youth is a stage of development of the human body, from birth to puberty to majority, until the end of school. During this time the body grows and gains strength; and, at the same time, the senses and attributes develop. During this time parents and educators are responsible for the rearing and deeds of children who have not yet reached legal age. But once the child completes school and becomes independent and enters the labor force or a chosen profession, he then becomes responsible for his own deeds, thoughts and feelings. From this time on the child produces his own fateful causes and consequences. In the early years, until puberty, all the elements work on the growth of the human body, especially the Earth element, which regulates the body's growth.

Aging is actually a phase of the human body's death process, due to the decomposing activities of the elements, especially the Earth element. This stage expresses itself through the decrease of energy, through irregularities and frequent disturbances of the function of individual elements and through ailments.

21. What is a beautiful body from the Hermetic point of view?

From the Hermetic point of view, a beautiful body is a beautiful shell, a garment of the eternal spirit, who uses it as an instrument of expression on the physical plane. A beautiful body is also a symbol and expression of total health, of unison and complete harmony of all the elemental powers that are active in a human being.

22. How can the body be impregnated or prepared?

We can impregnate the physical body with various wishes, attributes and abilities by drawing into the body those universal elements that correspond to our wishes, prayers etc. We place into these elements the circumstances, capabilities, attributes and powers with which we would like to ennoble and impregnate our body. All our wishes, capabilities and attributes must correspond with our development. The impregnation is accomplished by means of the Akasha principle, which expresses itself effectively through the electromagnetic fluid or the particular elements that belong to it.

23. What is the significance of the electromagnetic dynamic in the human organism?

The electromagnetic dynamic is a steady harmonious tension between the electric and magnetic fluids. The effectiveness of this dynamic depends upon the emanation of power from both poles, the electric and magnetic fluids. The active or electric pole equals activity, the passive or magnetic pole equals inactivity.

24. How do the elements work in the human organism?
The elements work in the human organism through their functions and powers. The Fire element is at work in the head, where everything active takes place. In the chest the Air element dominates through automatic breathing. In the abdominal area the Water element is predominant, which decomposes and eliminates all liquids, followed by the Earth element, which through its firmness holds together the entire body with bones, muscles and flesh. This element is also responsible for the growth, maturity and death of the physical body. Besides that, specific elements exist in every organ and body part and complete the harmony.

25. What is the "golden mean" of the body — the Akasha?
The "golden mean" of the body is the Akasha point; it is the point of absolute equilibrium, the absolute depth point in the center of the body. From this central point the Akasha principle controls the entire physical body on the physical plane. This point is also called the solar plexus and is located between the spinal column and the pit of the stomach.

26. What causes the growth of the body?
The growth of the body is regulated through breathing and the digestion of nourishment, the so-called combustion process. Sleep, rest and movement are also absolutely necessary. In actuality, we are dealing here with the work of the tetrapolar magnet in its correspondence with the elements, by which they nourish and strengthen themselves so that they can perform their functions properly.

27. How does karma affect the human body?
Negative karma expresses itself in the human body through particular ailments that cannot be healed as long as the effects of the karma last.

28. The moon's influence upon menstruation.
The electric fluid, which is very effective throughout the waxing of the moon but strongest at the time of the full moon, has a particular cleansing influence upon the blood of a woman. Between the magnetic fluid of the moon and the electric fluid in the blood of the woman, a particular tension develops which binds the clean blood that is capable of impregnation. The impurities formed in the blood during the course of this tension are separated from the clean blood and evacuated from the body through the woman's eliminatory organs. This is the effect of induction, the regular rhythm.

29. What is mental fertility?
Mental fertility is a perfectly realized imagination through which, by means of belief, will and concentration, we can achieve everything.

30. What is life and what is death?
Life is the eternal work of the elements in the tetrapolar magnet. Everything is born, prospers, matures and dies. It is the cycle of life, of existence, in the evolution of everything created. The physical death of a human being is merely a transition of the spiritual and astral bodies into the astral plane after the life-cord, the astral matrix which connects the astral body to the physical body, is severed through the decomposing work of the elements.

31. What happens to the physical body when it is buried or cremated?
The physical body of the deceased person breaks down into the original elemental substances out of which it was created.

32. The various healing methods for maintaining one's own health.
We distinguish the following healing methods:

1. Healing through diet, to be used for minor disturbances of the elements in the body.

2. Natural healing: compresses, poultices or hot packs, massages, electrotherapy, baths, diet, sun-baths, water or hydrotherapy, air, physical exercises, plants or phytotherapy.

3. The official medical art, which heals in accordance with its special methods.

4. Allopathy, which heals with substances or active agents that are the opposite of the ones that caused the ailment.

5. Homeopathy, which heals with substances that are the same or similar to the ones which originally caused the ailment.

6. Electrotherapy, which heals with surplus electric fluid.

7. Electro-homeopathy, which heals with the electric or magnetic fluids of the Magnetopath.

8. Biochemistry, which heals with medications produced from living organic substances.

9. Spagyric medicine, which heals with remedies produced from plants.

10. In the field of Hermetic healing there are many other healing methods. All of these methods pursue only one goal: to re-establish the disturbed equilibrium of particular elements in the human body and thereby remove the ailment.

33. Different kinds of fluid condensers.
We differentiate the following kinds of fluid condensers:

1. Solid condensers made from metals.
2. Liquid condensers: tinctures.
3. Airy condensers: fragrances.

Furthermore, there are simple condensers made from, for example: chamomile, Russian black tea and sage. These condensers serve the development or influencing of the astral senses by means of the elements. Universal fluid condensers are composed of many plant extracts, which serve to influence the materia. There are also solid fluid condensers made from metals which, among other things, are used in the production of a magic mirror.

34. How do time and space behave towards the body?
Time and space are effective in the material or physical plane, so that a human being in his physical body gains the experience of limitations. This experience belongs to the conditions of one's life in the third dimension and to the totality of his mental, astral and physical existence.

35. Why do we lose the memory or knowledge of our previous lives?
We lose the memory of our past lives so that we may considerably improve upon our fate or destiny in our present development. If we were to possess the knowledge of our past lives, we would possess the knowledge of how to balance certain causes, and if we were to offset these causes, we would live a stereotypical life. Also, we would have no interest in life.

36. By what means is destiny or the duration of our physical life determined?
A karmic law stipulates: "As ye sow, so shall ye reap." This means that every human being produces certain causes through certain feelings, deeds and thoughts that are automatically and accurately recorded in the causal sphere and the physical, astral and

mental spheres. Every cause calls forth a corresponding effect or consequence related to the cause, whether in a positive sense, as when we are dealing with a positive cause, or in a negative sense when we are dealing with a negative cause. The negative consequences are the ones which we have to pay off, or, in other words, which we have to correct during our life on earth.

This is why everyone's life is controlled by the most sublime karmic law, and why the life span of every human being is exactly determined so that he can correct certain negative causes through good deeds and causes. For this purpose, destiny places a person into the appropriate circumstances, society and environment through which he may successfully improve himself. For this purpose he is given hundreds upon hundreds of opportunities to fulfill his primary objective in life.

As a general rule, the love of Universal Providence goes so far as to prolong the life of a human being when he enters upon the path of magical development, and Universal Providence will also prolong the life of a person who is heading towards absolute truth. A person's life span is always determined or dependent upon the ennoblement and perfection of the spirit, soul and body, because that is in fact the principal goal of human life. And sooner or later everyone must reach this state.

37. How do the mental and the astral express themselves through the five senses of the human organism?

The mental expresses itself on the physical plane through written and spoken thoughts or through pictures and concepts.

The astral expresses itself in the physical plane through passion, bad habits and negative attributes, or through the expression of positive attributes such as love, honesty, righteousness, work and art of all kinds, in the positive sense, and with the appropriate nuances of feelings or emotions. For this, we usually employ all the senses of the physical body.

38. What kind of goals do Hermetics pursue?

Hermetics pursue the ennoblement and the perfection of human beings in accordance with the universal laws of the macro- and microcosm and its correspondences, and to a greater or lesser degree in philosophical respects.

39. How does one-sided development or one-sided practice express itself if the practitioner does not follow the path of perfection?

One-sided development and one-sided exercises do not concur with the path of perfection; they increase one's elemental imbalance, weaken one's health and shorten one's life. Consequently, the functions of particular elements are abnormally increased or developed, whereas the functions of other elements are neglected, stunted or retarded.

40. Proper religion versus fanaticism.
Proper religion is the initiate's own particular universal view, which he forms through deep meditation and by becoming acquainted with the universal laws. That is the genuine universal religion.

Religious fanaticism distinguishes itself through exaggerated views in respect to questions of the church, or in respect to truths and convictions which, except for the fundamental idea of the existence of God, are always relative. Religious fanaticism expresses itself through fanatical human beings who cripple their bodies deliberately or who deny necessary nourishment to their bodies by extremely ascetic fasting, etc.

41. The relationship between God and a human being.
Every person is created in the image of God. Whosoever has understood this idea properly understands that a part of the Universal Providence rests within each human being. This is why a person endeavors to draw closer to his God and eventually to identify himself with Him. He achieves this through the realization of the divine idea within himself, beginning at the most fundamental level and then ascending, level by level, until he reaches the highest stage of union with God.

The great majority of believers do not know their God. He is simply worshiped and loved by them; He is a support for them, because Divine Providence represents the purity of all ideas and this purity is reflected in a person's attributes, his consciousness and conscience. A human being arranges his life in accordance with these things.

42. The attitude of the student towards his teacher.
A student should honor, respect and love his teacher or master above all, for he knows that his teacher has been called upon by Universal Providence to educate and teach him the divine ideas and aspects as well as the universal laws in the macro-and microcosm, those great mysteries in the cosmos and in a human being that are hidden to the eyes of those who are not called.

For the student, a master is an aspect or representative of Divine Providence itself which has become personified in the master and which speaks to the student by means of the master's being. That is how sublime the master is in regards to the student, and that is the esteem in which a good student holds his master, his teacher.

43. What a teacher can do and what he cannot.
A teacher who educates a student can enlighten the student's intellect and consciousness so that the student makes better progress on the path to the highest goal. This happens in the following manner: the student makes a connection with the consciousness of his master, or the master himself enlightens the student with his wisdom by transferring an enlightenment of consciousness to the student. This enables the stu-

dent to comprehend the spiritual and astral problems connected with his own development much more easily.

The master cannot change the student's character, because he cannot substantiate such a deed to Universal Providence. Every human being changes his character through the kind of life he lives, all in accordance with the universal laws; the development of a human being and the karmic laws are all subject to universal laws. If the master were to change the student's character in spite of all this, he would have to carry the consequences; in other words he would take over a part of the student's karmic debts, depending upon the degree to which he has changed or improved the student's character. The master may, however, teach the student the manner in which he himself can best improve his character.

44. The difference between perfection and holiness.
There is an immense difference between perfection and holiness. A perfect human being is absolutely in balance in regards to the elements, and his soul is impregnated with the highest divine virtues that correspond to the four universal elements. Such an individual has achieved identification and union with God in his soul.

A holy person is still imperfect, because he has realized only one divine attribute within himself and he is merely holy, untouchable. This is why he must continue to return to the earthly plane until he has become perfected.

45. The concept of God.
In His innermost and most concealed Being, God resembles the uncreated light. This highest of aspects is unfathomable; it is inconceivable and unimaginable through our external and internal senses. Esoterically, a human being is describing the Akasha whenever he uses the word God. God is therefore the Akashic or so-called Etheric principle, the primordial existence, the first cause of all things and of everything created. He is the primordial power, the fifth power which has created everything, which controls everything and keeps everything in an equilibrium. God is the beginning and the purity of all thoughts and ideas. He is the causal world in which everything created maintains itself, from the highest to the lowest spheres. He is the quintessence of the alchemists. He is the all-in-all.

Divine Providence can also be found in human beings; within them it is best reflected in their attributes and capabilities. An awakened person who knows and masters the universal laws of the macro- and microcosm knows very well that he is a part of the divine Self. Therefore he considers it his holy duty to become one with God on the magical and Hermetic path. This is why he forms the highest divine idea of a personal God Whom he worships and loves above all and to Whom he aspires upward, step by step, from the lowest to the highest level, by completing the divine ideas or, in other words, by identification with his personal divinity. The average human being does not know his God; that is why he can only believe in Him. He worships and loves Him so that he can find support in Him and so that he does not lose himself.

46. What are the macrocosm and the microcosm?
The macrocosm is an expression of God in the created light. It came into being from the Akasha principle through the effects of the four elements — Fire, Water, Air and Earth.

The microcosm is the human being in which the macrocosm is reflected. Everything that is present in the universe on a large scale can be found in a human being, in the microcosm. The human being was also created from the Akasha principle through the reciprocal effects of the elements in the tetrapolar magnet. Therefore a human being is the true image of God.

47. The Hermetic significance of occult analogies.
Occult analogies are true replicas of all expressions of nature in a human being, corresponding to the tetrapolar magnet.

48. Symbolism in nature.
Symbolism is the language of nature. We make use of this language through various pictures, numbers, colors, signs and sounds. We use symbols to express certain secrets that should remain hidden from those who are not chosen. Nature itself speaks to us through this language, mostly in dreams while we are asleep. The Kabbalistic Tree of Life is an example of sublime symbolism. Any matter, passion, event, being, etc., can be expressed symbolically in a certain corresponding manner. Therefore it is in the interest of every Hermetic to at least familiarize himself with the most important symbols of nature and the effectiveness of the universal elements.

49. The ten fundamental truths of the Divine ideas.
Why do human beings have ten fingers?
Here are the ten fundamental truths:
1. God, the highest divine principle.
2. Love.
3. Wisdom.
4. Omnipotence.
5. Omniscience.
6. Lawfulness.
7. Eternal Life.
8. Omnipresence.
9. Immortality.
10. The purity of all ideas and thoughts.

The five fingers on a person's right hand indicate that the five universal elements — Fire, Air, Water, Earth and Akasha — prevail within him in accordance with the emanation of their active polarity.

The middle finger in particular corresponds to the Akasha principle, which is the highest principle and which maintains and controls the four elements of the other fingers.

The five fingers on the left hand also express the five universal elements in the same sequence. But on this hand the elements emanate the effectiveness of their negative poles.

The index finger represents Fire, the thumb Water, the middle finger the Akasha principle, the ring finger Earth, and the little finger Air; the right hand represents the positive and the left hand the negative polarity of the elements.

50. What is meant by the genius concept of God?
The genius concept of God is that of the universal eternal sun, absolute perfection, effective without time and space.

51. The world of ideas and the causal world.
The world of ideas is the mental plane of the highest Akasha principle, which is the basis of the ideas of all thoughts. The causal world is the Etheric principle on all planes; every trace, every step a human being has ever made has been recorded there from the thoughts, feelings and deeds that occurred on all planes during the time of his mortal life.

The Function of The Akasha

1. What is rhythm in the material world or material body?
We understand rhythm as an interruption of the electric and magnetic fluids that work within us both inductively and deductively as well as working outside of us in the material world. Inductively the interruption is effective from the inside to the outside and deductively from the outside to the inside. The interruption may take place either regularly or irregularly. If the interruptions are in regular intervals we achieve a balanced influence, whereas chaos is the result if the interruptions are irregular. The slowing down or speeding up of the rhythm depends upon short or long waves. The longer the waves, the milder their effect; the shorter the waves, the more penetrating their effect. This is the secret of magical dynamics, the quadrature of the circle.

2.   How does rhythm express itself?
Rhythm expresses itself within us through breathing — inductively through inhalation and deductively through exhalation. The labor of the heart in the human body is also an inductive and deductive interruption, the rhythm of life and movement. The activities of consciousness while awake and the activities of the subconscious while asleep are also manifestations of the rhythm of life.

The succession of day and night, the constant repetitive activity of nature — namely spring, summer, autumn and winter — the orbits of planets and stars, any sound, song, speech, or music, any movement is an expression of the rhythm of life in the material world.

3.   What is induction from the Hermetic point of view?
Induction is the foundation of the rhythm of life; it induces the interruption. At the same time, we are dealing with a law of physics, namely electricity and magnetism.

4.   The Hermetic significance of introspection.
The Hermetic significance of proper introspection consists of continuously extending and maintaining the elemental equilibrium of all the elements on all the planes that are effective within us until we reach the absolute elemental equilibrium. This elemental equilibrium guarantees the total health and vitality which we require for our magical ascent. At the same time all the universal energies of all the elements can express themselves within us, through which we can continue to develop ourselves astrally and spiritually.

5.   The Divine Judgment.
      Who is the guardian of the astral realm?
Divine judgment is actually a strict accounting of our positive and negative deeds which takes place as soon as we have reached the end of our mortal life and arrive at the threshold of the astral realm. The guardian of the astral region is the Akasha principle, which accurately and precisely assesses our thoughts, feelings and deeds in accordance with cause and effect and then, as long as we are not yet completely in balance, determines our subsequent destiny.

6.   How does the Akasha principle express itself in an average human being and in a Hermetic?
In the case of an average human being the Akasha principle expresses itself in the consciousness, and in the case of a Hermetic in the self-consciousness, in the becoming conscious of who he is.

7. What is matter from the Hermetic point of view?
Matter is the result of the labor of the elements and the electromagnetic fluid, all of which originate from the Akasha principle. Matter exists in time and space, has measure and weight. In matter, the electric and magnetic fluids are active.

8. What is the transmutation of matter?
The transmutation of matter consists of alchemically changing the composition of the atomic nucleus and elements into the substance of another element. What is given consideration is the electromagnetic fluid, which is contained in the substance and which can be influenced in a particular manner so that the matter changes in its fundamentals.

9. The Philosophers' Stone.
The philosophers' stone is a wonderful fluid condenser, an elixir, the red tincture, the so-called green lion, in which is contained the concentrated energy from all four elements in such an amount that it not only heals all ailments, balances and increases our vitality, but also completely rejuvenates the entire body. This elixir is very rarely used by initiates because it has a great disadvantage to those who use it. Not only does the person rejuvenate physically, but also astrally and spiritually; therefore he loses all the experiences he has gained and which, through long years of strenuous labor, he has accumulated with great effort.

10. The beings of the elements, their functions and effects upon matter.
The beings of the elements live in the astral world. When they are given a certain task and work for the magician upon the material plane, they have an effect only upon the physical substance, provided of course that the magician has given them enough of his own vital and astral energy so that they can condense themselves as matter.

11. Four laws of the effectiveness of matter.
Matter is effective in time and space, in weight and measure.

12. What is Maya and what is its function?
According to Hindu philosophy, Maya is the world of delusion. What we are discussing here is the physical world, whose responsibility it is to carefully conceal the secrets of the universal laws in the macro- and microcosm from people who are undeserving.

In reality the world of delusion exists only for those who do not know the universal laws. For the initiate, these delusions are merely obstacles which he easily recognizes, which he can explain, and which he opposes until he removes them completely.

13. What difference exists between mysticism and Kabbalah, Magic and Hermetics?

A mystic, unless he is also a magician, approaches God through an all-encompassing love; a magician chooses to make the approach through the path of the will and control. There is of course no difference between mysticism and magic when it comes to the initiation itself, because an initiated magician is generally a mystic as well.

Magic and Kabbalah are the highest sciences that exist. Hermetic philosophy solves questions regarding God, humanity and the cosmos in a more or less philosophical manner. The concept of Hermetics is interpreted in literature in various ways and is attributed to Hermes Trismegistus, among others. Magic is a practical science which corresponds to the highest art form, while the Kabbalah is founded strictly and exactly upon the highest cognizance, all-encompassing wisdom and science.

14. How do beings from the interplanetary planes view a human being who occupies himself with Hermetics?

The interplanetary beings view a Hermetic as a perfect interplanetary being who can clearly be distinguished from ordinary human beings through his clear, radiating aura.

15. The distribution and application of the Solomonic Temple to the mental, astral and material.

The four fundamental pillars of the Solomonic Temple are knowledge, courage, volition and silence. In the mental plane we become aware of these four attributes; we meditate on them and then transform them into deeds.

We cultivate knowledge through our daily studies, through the repetition of the universal laws of the macro- and microcosm. We make a firm determination in the spirit to cultivate courage and volition within us, convinced that we already possess them. When it comes to silence, we remain in the astral plane in our thoughts, a state that can be achieved through vacancy of mind.

We condense knowledge in the astral plane through the neutrality of the Air element. We imagine that all cognitions of truth, all the knowledge of the laws of the macro- and microcosm are already deeply impressed upon our memory so that we take this with us for eternity and so that it remains forever in our possession. Usually, knowledge is expressed through speech; in the astral plane this occurs in the practical sense through thinking out loud.

Courage grows in the astral plane through the effects of the Fire element. It belongs to the element of Fire and it increases so long as we always imagine that there is sufficient might and energy contained in our courage to overcome the most difficult obstacles and reach our goals at any cost.

We condense volition in the astral plane through magnetism. This attribute belongs to the universal Water element; we imagine that everything we want to achieve

— solely for noble purposes, of course — has already become a reality as soon as we become aware of it.

We consolidate silence in the astral plane and we secure it through a firm determination not to disclose anything we consider to be a Holy Secret and through which we are bound by an oath — neither in thought nor feeling, much less in deed, not even in a dream. We have sworn this oath ourselves in front of the Universal Providence through our master or teacher. These dynamics come into being through the tension and influence of the electromagnetic fluid of the Earth element, wherein the active and passive pole is effective. In this manner we have condensed all four pillars.

Through preparation, the attributes and powers are condensed on the astral plane to such a degree that they can be transferred to the material plane via the astral matrix.

Knowledge projected to the outside expresses itself in the material plane as speech, in considerations or thoughts spoken aloud or transferred to paper. While in this state of development, consciousness envelops itself in sound, speech, writing and motion, in other words in a certain rhythm (in the interruption of the electric current and magnetism). And when it has materialized, it is in this form that it is most effective.

Courage, which we have developed on the mental and astral planes, brings us material fruit. We achieve everything that ennobles us and leads us to our highest goal with a firm will, with the power of the imagination and manifested belief. It is a creative act in which the Creator is reflected in us.

Volition manifests as deeds in the physical plane; that which we intended to do becomes a reality. The energy of the magnetic fluid is so mightly charged that it has to discharge with the active part of the Fire element — in other words, with the electric fluid through which it became effective.

Silence is a power that is expressed on all planes by every magician who understands how to keep silent. If a magician understands how to keep silent in thoughts and feelings, he will also be qualified to keep silence on the material plane, where there are particularly severe conditions placed upon silence, especially in front of people who do not have the calling. Should this power of silence become strongly condensed on the material plane through the effectiveness of the electromagnetic fluid and through frequent obstacles of the Earth element, it may become absolute taciturnity. Through this, its might also grows automatically in the material plane.

16. What animates, stimulates and dulls the senses in the human body?

All senses in the human body are stimulated through exercises that properly correspond to those senses. The senses are dulled by artificial stimulants such as narcotics, tobacco, and alcohol, and by severely over-dimensionalizing a strongly condensed element, an elemental substance. We also dull our senses if, for example, we look into the sun without protective glasses or condense a certain element within ourselves very strongly and keep it within us, or if we drink too much alcohol or coffee etc.

17. What is the material aura in the material body and in the physical world?
The material aura is the sum of radiating colored attributes, and it shows itself in everything that is created on earth. We are dealing here with the visible effects of the working elements of the tetrapolar magnet in the physical plane. At the same time, the aura in the physical body represents the colored radiating elementary effects, or rather the labor of the tetrapolar magnet. As far as its quality is concerned, this radiation of the material aura corresponds exactly with the aura of the astral body.

18. What is Brahma's breathing?
Brahma's breathing is the respiration of life, which God the Creator has created by breathing His vital energy or vitality and life into everything created.

19. Distribution of the electromagnetic influences during the course of the day and their practical employment and application.
The effectiveness, influence, and dominance of a particular element changes every twenty-four minutes. This is the sequence:

From 0 to 24 minutes	Akasha
From 25 to 48 minutes	Air
From 49 to 72 minutes	Fire
From 73 to 96 minutes	Earth
From 97 to 120 minutes	Water

*The above cycle begins at midnight.

A complete cycle of the predominant elements (tattvas) takes two hours, and then it begins again. You will be most successful with the optical exercises while the Fire element is predominant, with the acoustical exercises when Air is predominant, with feeling or sentience exercises when Water is predominant, and with the exercises which increase one's consciousness when Earth is predominant — in other words, practicing smell and taste in combination with the optical, acoustic and sentience exercises. During the predominance of Akasha, you will be most successful with the negative state and also becoming conscious or aware of everything present, the "Eternal Now."

If we wish to achieve greater success, or if we wish to achieve success in a magical task, we should practice these exercises in accordance with the aforementioned timetable for the appropriate elements.

20. *What is sin?*
Sin is a mistake we make when we violate the laws of the macro- and microcosm. When we know we are doing something wrong and do it anyway, we are making a serious mistake, committing a sin.

21. *What is the sin against the Holy Ghost?*
A magician commits a sin against the Holy Ghost if, for example, he consciously breaks his word or an oath he has sworn in front of Universal Providence, for whatever reason.

A sin against the Holy Ghost is a conscious violation of the universal laws by the magician in the worst way and in particularly serious cases.

22. *Why are initiates sent to our earthly plane and what is their mission?*
Initiates are sent to the earthly plane to accomplish something noble for humankind. Every true initiate has a particular mission — for example, to educate students in the magical arts and sciences, to heal those who are afflicted with incurable diseases, to give an account of the absolute truth of the universal laws of the macro- and microcosm, to prevent particular catastrophes, to write books about wisdom and the perfect path to God etc.

23. *What would it mean to disclose knowledge and discoveries (inventions) ahead of their appointed time on the material plane?*
It would be an illegal intervention in the developmental law of humankind to disclose knowledge and discoveries before their appointed time. The developmental law is an aspect of the karmic law of cause and effect, which is the highest and most sublime law. Therefore it must be respected by every magician absolutely and unconditionally.

24. *Why do new diseases constantly arise, and what is their origin?*
Being faced with the fact that medical science has been successful in healing many severe diseases, karmic law reacts to these successful interventions with new ailments, so that we human beings do not escape the natural equilibrium of causes that come into being by themselves. We are dealing here with both the karmic and the developmental processes at the same time.

These ailments come into being in the human body through the disturbance of the function of the elements. The disturbance of the elemental functions comes into being primarily through severely derailed negative attributes, passions, and bad habits which we have nourished with repetition, and also through physical causes such as, for example, colds, burns or accidents etc. Every ailment is of course an elemental imbalance of the karmic burden from an earlier life.

25. What is fatigue and what is the physiological procedure in the body that causes it?
If the Earth element in a person dominates or becomes more effective, then the entire body becomes fatigued. We are dealing here with a temporary disturbance of the electromagnetic fluid in the human body. Overloading the nerves and muscles causes a general fatigue.

26. The effectiveness of the nerves and the circumstances under which they become overloaded.
The nerves are the main factor affecting all our senses. Their main center is in the brain and in the spinal cord. Every sense is connected with the nerves to the head or brain like an electric wire with its main center. Sensual perception takes place through the sensual organs upon the path of the nerves to the brain where we become aware of what we perceive.

However, the nerves are weakened if they are overloaded in one way or another. For example, the eyes may become overloaded through a light that is too strong, the ears through a sound that is too loud; burning or injury to the nerves may occur anywhere in the body. The nerves can become ill and exert a harmful influence upon our health and our senses. Also, various ailments can have a harmful and disturbing influence upon the nerves and the senses.

27. How does an imbalance express itself in the mental, astral, and material regions?
An elemental imbalance expresses itself in the mental region through negative attributes and ailments of the spirit; such imbalances are not sufficiently condensed to manifest or transfer to the astral region.

An elemental imbalance develops in the astral region through negative attributes and ailments which are projected into a situation.

In the material region, ailments develop through expressions of negative attributes, passions and bad habits as far as language, feelings and thoughts are concerned, and they are transferred as mature effects into the material region from the astral region. Negative attributes and powers are radiating effects of the elements and originate from their negative poles. All together, they express themselves as the physical, astral and mental aura.

FOREWORD
The Great Arcanum

The nine charts of virtues and passions included in this new edition of *Franz Bardon: Questions & Answers — The Great Arcanum*, in accordance with the four elements, the *Yod-He Vau-He*, explain cause, effect, and consequence in the good (positive) sense and in the bad (negative) sense, as well as qualities and quantities in their active-positive and passive-negative forms.

All ailments, physical and astral, originate from our carnal desires, which are the cause of all our failures, because they are passions. Translated, "passions" means "sufferings," therefore, the cause of all failures and sufferings occur when we follow our passions. Pride is the most destructive passion, love the most constructive virtue. Not only does this apply individually, but also to families, groups of people, nations, and to an even greater extent to our planet. Whatever applies to the microcosm, our body, soul, and spirit also applies to the macrocosm, our planet.

Through passions, mankind is also responsible for our weather and related catastrophes by making changes in nature, e.g., deforestation causes severe storms, rain, etc., and activities such as drilling shafts into the ground for oil and gas eventually cause fires that cannot be contained and which level entire areas, populated and unpopulated. The weather is also subject to the four elements as is everything else.

If you have attempted the exercises in the Bardon books, and tried to succeed again and again and you stopped and started the practice, you will find the causes for your lack of success in these charts.

An imbalance [ailment] of the soul is caused by passions; this imbalance can cause a person to become a murderer, a thief, a liar, etc. If we made the effort, then those people who are afflicted with these ailments of the soul could be healed. But instead of being helped, they are punished. That is why thousands of years ago judges were appointed to help these people, and not to incarcerate or dispense death sentences to those whose souls are ill. Any person or nation that possesses pride is always at war and is therefore afflicted with the most severe soul-ailments possible.

The following is an excerpt from *Initiation into Hermetics*, which points out what is required by our body, and which also applies to the macrocosm.

> *Our entire life depends upon the continuous supply of burnable substances, that is, from nourishment and through breathing. A supply of various kinds of nourishment, which contain the fundamental substances of the elements is advisable, so that every element receives the necessary substances for its preservation. If we were dependent throughout our entire lives upon one kind of nourishment, our bodies would definitely become ill; that is, a disharmony would be caused in the body. Through the decomposition of nourishment and*

air, the elements are supplied with the substances that maintain them, and their activity is also sustained in this manner. That is the natural way of life for a human being. Should one or another element lack the necessary energy-substance or fuel, there would be an immediate reaction. This lack manifests itself in the functions, which are affected by it. For example,

> *when the Fire element in the body reaches a higher level of effectiveness due to a lack of nourishment among other elements, we feel thirsty;*
> *when the Air element becomes more effective, we feel hungry;*
> *when the Water element becomes more effective, we feel cold; and*
> *when the Earth element becomes more effective, we feel tired.*

A satiation of the elements in the body calls forth intensified effects in the particular area. Should there be a preponderance: of the Fire element: the body feels a yearning for movement and activity ensues; of the Air element: the body curbs the intake of any food; of the Water element: the process of elimination increases; an the Earth element: manifests itself in the aspects of one's sex life, but it does not necessarily express itself through the sex drive in the carnal sense. It can manifest externally, for example in the elderly mostly though an urge for increased physical activity or creative work.

☙❧

Therefore, if you want to be in control of your body and soul, you must be in control of your passions and eliminate the worst one, otherwise, you will not have the energy to do the exercises in Bardon's works, and you will fail repeatedly. The very least you must do is to have your passions in the proper order, as for instance, the Fire element 21 negative attributes, Air element 20, Water element 19, Earth element 18. In other words, you must purify and cleanse yourself of your passions.

The negative character traits reflected in these charts are the cause of all of mankind's ailments and woes, individually and collectively. Replacing them with positive character traits will eliminate all ailments, which are considered curable or incurable, as well as all other problems and predicaments.

This can be accomplished quite easily if and when an individual, or a nation, spends his time productively on getting well, rather than embracing and maintaining his or her ailments by administering poison; everyone who is ill would get well, because there is only one way a person can kill himself or be killed, and that is through passions.

However, nowadays the entire focus of individuals and nations is directed toward remaining sick by embracing ailments instead of health. The reason for this is that health is not profitable but illness and death are. That is why truth has the smallest audience, but plenty of enemies.

In conclusion, Franz Bardon provided these newly-found charts to his students in Prague. For every student to use them effectively requires no further instruction or explanation, as everything has been thoroughly explained by Franz Bardon in *Initiation into Hermetics.*

Fire Element — Jod י in Hebrew

Divine fundamental attribute	Omnipotence and all-encompassing energy (will)
Qualities of the Fire element (electric fluid)	Hot, dry and expansive
Signs of the Zodiac	♈ Aries ♌ Leo ♐ Sagittarius
Planetary Spheres	☉ Sun = number 6, ♂ Mars = number 5
Organ of Perception	Eye (vision)
Temperament	Choleric

Positive Light-Day	Negative Darkness-Night
1. Willpower, strength of the will, the force and the might of the will.	1. (a) Abuse of power toward animals and human beings, destructive urge, sadism, arson, murder (causes: envy, jealousy, etc.). (b) Excess Water element: Weak will, powerless (depression), suicide.
2. Determination, power of self-assertion.	2. Indecision, vacillation (weakness, cowardice) shyness.
3. Self-control: Strict toward oneself.	3. (a) Lack of self-control (externally) = rage, fury, anger, quarrelsomeness, thirst for revenge, hate, urge to annihilate, madness, passion, fanaticism. (b) Lack of self-control (internally) = weakness, self-torment (fanaticism), self-torture and masochism (misguided self-knowledge).
4. Perseverance (endurance). Tenacious when pursuing a goal.	4. Weakness, instability, scattered thoughts and energy, resignation.
5. Desire or urge for freedom, internally and externally.	5. No freedom, slavery: Dependence on sensual and material urges and craving for human beings and objects.
6. Boldness, daring.	6. (a) Exuberance, recklessness. (b) Fear, dread leads to cowardice.
7. Diligence, activity, assiduity.	7. (a) Restlessness, frantic pace, hyperactivity. (b) Indifference, laziness, passivity, apathy, lethargy.
8. Enthusiasm, joy.	8. (a) Effusiveness, overly excited, hysteria. (b) Disinterest, dullness.
9. Conscious of the present (see Earth element, conscious of the present).	9. (a) Confusion, inattentiveness. (b) Lethargy and tiredness.
10. Active helpfulness, social cooperation.	10. Indifference and carelessness toward our fellowman, social inactivity.

Air Element — He ה in Hebrew

Divine Fundamental Attribute	All-encompassing wisdom and omniscience
Qualities of the Air element (neutral fluid)	Warm and moist, light and weightless (Intellect, intelligence)
Signs of the Zodiac	♊ Gemini ♎ Libra ♒ Aquarius
Planetary Spheres	♃ Jupiter = number 4, ☿ Mercury = number 8.
Organ of Perception	Ear (hearing)
Temperament	Sanguine

Positive	Negative
1. Interest in human beings, the world and the cosmos.	1. Indifference.
2. Thirst for knowledge, willingness to learn = discernment, ability to judge.	2. Mental or intellectual laziness, satisfied with ignorance, unwilling to learn leading = lack of judgment.
3. Courage is the balance between carelessness, fear, and cowardice (level-headedness, caution).	3. (a) Boisterousness, foolhardiness, carelessness, negligence, rashness, thoughtlessness, impulsiveness. (b) Angst, fear, cowardice, paranoia, resignation, depression, fickleness.
4. Striving for wisdom, spiritual perfection, idealism, knowledge of oneself leads to self-control. Asceticism.	4. Satisfied with imperfection, indifferent toward one's own imperfection. Laziness and indolence.
5. Recognizing and observing the laws of Karma. Reducing karmic debt through positive activities in a mental, astral and physical respect, resulting in spiritual progress.	5. Not acknowledging or observing the karmic laws. Karmic inactivity and/or negative activities in a mental, astral and physical respect. Result is spiritual stagnation or regression.
6. Do not criticize or condemn other people or conditions (e.g., I did not create the world and human beings. I must assess them, but not condemn them).	6. Urge to criticize. Criticizing and/or condemning other people, natural occurrences and so on (e.g., I would have created the world differently).
7. Truthfulness, honesty.	7. Lies, untruthfulness, calumny, boasting or bragging.
8. Objectivity, realism, truth, truthfulness.	8. (a) Overestimating one's own powers and abilities. Prejudice, subjectivity. (b) Carelessness, underestimation, mistakes and lies (due to angst and cowardice).
9. Optimism, humor, joy.	9. (a) Effusiveness, illusionism, overexcitement. (b) Pessimism, melancholy, depression, lack of humor.
10. Tolerance, magnanimity, generosity, good-naturedness.	10. Intolerance, pettiness, stinginess, maliciousness.

11. Skillfulness, adaptability.	11. (a) Ineptitude, superficiality. (b) Inflexibility, clumsiness.
12. Watchfulness, astuteness.	12. (a) Inattentiveness, lack of concentration. (b) Sleepiness, apathy.

Water Element — Vau ו in Hebrew

Divine Fundamental Attribute	All-encompassing love (eternal life)
Qualities of the Water element (magnetic fluid)	Cold and moist
Signs of the Zodiac	♋ Cancer ♏ Scorpio ♓ Pisces
Planetary Spheres	☽ Moon (Life) = number 9, ♀ Venus (Love) = number 7
Organ of Perception	Feelings (skin)
Temperament	Melancholy

Positive	Negative
1. Respect, friendliness, sympathy with the world (human beings and nature).	1. Contempt, unfriendliness, antipathy. (Possible causes: stupidity, prejudice, overly sensitive, weak self-awareness).
2. Love for your fellowman, altruism, kindness, forgiveness.	2. Emotional frigidity, indifference, jealousy, envy, antipathy leads to hate which leads to a destructive urge.
3. Erotic moderation leads to spiritual love, chastity and purity (for the pure everything is pure; love is the law when love is subject to the will).	3. Erotic immoderation and excess, sensuous love, lasciviousness, perversity, sadism, masochism.
4. Sensitivity, sympathy, compassion, emotional warmth.	4. Apathy, superficiality, emotional frigidity, mercilessness.
5. Seriousness, dignity, devotion, honor, respect = reverence = worship.	5. Lack of seriousness, undignified, dishonorable, disregard leads to contempt.
6. Religiousness, respect and tolerance toward the religious and ideological conviction of other people.	6. Non-religious. Disregard for sacred relics and religious conviction of others, proselytizing leads to persecution of those with a different mind-set.
7. Gratitude and respect for a true spiritual leader (Guru) or Master. Support of the Master's work leads to reduction of karma, which leads to spiritual progress.	7. Ingratitude = egotism + stupidity and disregard for a Master or Guru. Not supporting Master's work = no reduction of karma = spiritual stagnation!
8. Modesty, humility, making do with what one has. (A person who has little, not a wealthy person who has much!)	8. Immodesty, arrogance, vanity, squandering, greed, avarice.

9. Forgiveness, understanding, friendliness.	9. Vindictiveness, rudeness, unfriendliness, brutality.
10. Patience, forbearance.	10. (a) Impatience, intolerance, irritability. (b) Apathy, dullness.
11. Trust, belief.	11. Distrust, lack of faith.

Earth Element — He ה in Hebrew

Divine Fundamental Attributes	All-encompassing consciousness, omnipresence ("I" consciousness)
Qualities of the Earth element (electro-magnetic fluid)	Cold and dry, dense and heavy
Signs of the Zodiac	♉Taurus ♍Virgo ♑Capricorn
Planetary Sphere	Earth (zone girdling the Earth) (Malchuth, in Hebrew) = 10 ♄Saturn (Akasha) = number 3
Organs of Perception	Tongue = taste, Nose = smell
Temperament	Phlegmatic
Positive	Negative
1. Consciousness, I-consciousness, self-confidence, survival instinct. (Self-consciousness or conscious of being awake.)	1. (a) Weakness of self (inferiority complex) = loss of oneself, giving up on oneself, dream-state, conscious of being asleep, medial state. (b) Callousness, egotism.
2. Self-confidence (through introspection), independence, equilibrium, security.	2. Weakness of self, lack of independence, relying on other people, insecurity.
3. Self-control, asceticism (mentally, astrally and physically). Self-control means controlling the physical!	3. Lack of control, lacking self-control, inability of introspection and asceticism.
4. Unselfishness, helpfulness, altruistic dealings with money and other valuables.	4. Selfishness, egotism, excessive striving for earthly goods, greed for money.
5. (a) Justice (justness), conscientiousness, caution. (b) Responsible toward creation (human beings, animals and environment and nature).	5. (a) Injustice, irresponsibility, carelessness. (b) Irresponsible toward creation (negligence and brutality toward mankind, animals and environment and nature).
6. Equanimity, calmness, objectivity, sobriety.	6. (a) Touchiness, irritability, nervousness. (b) Indifference, dullness.
7. Ability to concentrate in the spiritual and physical spheres, determination.	7. Lack of concentration, absent-mindedness, laziness, aimlessness.
8. Order, systematics, meticulousness, thoroughness, punctuality leads to reliability.	8. Disorder, lack of systematization, imperfection, superficiality, unpunctuality leads to unreliability.

9. Having to ability to resist. Firmness, endurance.	9. Weakness, instability, false leniency.
10. (a) Moderation in all phases of life. (b) Generous in matters concerning your fellowman.	10. (a) Excessive eating, drinking etc., squandering, a high opinion of oneself, arrogance, boasting. (b) Pettiness, stinginess, greed, rapacity.
11. Discretion.	11. Talkativeness, divulging secrets.
12. Freedom, unimpeachability, unassailability = invulnerability, imperturbability.	12. Inhibition (not free) = clinging to earthly goods and human beings, dependency = slavery, losing yourself, suicide.
13. Conscious of the present = keeping the present in the present.	13. Attaching your consciousness to events of the past or making plans for the future.
14. Wisdom (from knowledge and experience), equilibrium in all situations of life, skillfulness, the ability to judge through learning processes.	14. Lack of wisdom, lack of interest, ignorance, ineptitude, clumsiness. Know-it-all attitude = judging without knowledge.

Character Training in accordance with Franz Bardon's System
Chart of Qualities and Quantities

Overview				
Attributes and Energies (Qualities and Quantities) In all the elements and on all planes from a universal view				
A. Principles and Ideas				
	Description of Ideas and Principles Qualities or Attributes		Description of the Effects Quantities or Energies	
	Active-Positive	Passive-Negative	Active-Positive	Passive-Negative
1.	Akasha = All in All			
2.	Prana	Prana	Prana	Prana
3.	Emanation of the eternal, eternity.	Emanation of the eternal, eternity.	Akasha.	Akasha.
4.	You spend your time with positive spiritual work.	You squander your time with negative mental activities, and laziness.	Time, positive. How strong you appear in time. Energy of positive thoughts on the mental plane.	Time, negative. How strong you appear in time. The energy of negative thoughts on the mental plane.
5.	Useful life on the astral plane.	Useless life on the astral plane.	Measurement of space in the astral plane.	Measurement of space in the astral plane.

	Active-Positive	Passive-Negative	Active-Positive	Passive-Negative
6.	Attraction of the earth, justness, usefulness, positive activities on the physical plane.	Attraction of the earth, injustice, uselessness, negative activities on the physical plane.	Weight, measure, space, time in the material plane.	Weight, measure, space, time in the material plane.
7.	Law, karma.	Causes contrary to the karmic laws.	Fate, created causes, positive consequences.	Fate, created causes, negative consequences.
8.	Evolution, ennobling a human being.	Character deterioration.	Obstacles increase = growth of the human being materially, astrally and mentally and on all planes.	Decadence of the human being on all planes.
9.	Lawfulness, Analogy.	Directing one's activities against the law.	The effect of the universal laws.	Offences against the law. Negative effects.
10.	Justness (justice).	Injustice, mistakes, shortcomings.	Energy or the power (effect) of fate (karma).	Energy (effect) of the conscious or unconscious violation of the universal laws and analogies.
11.	Religion.	Atheism.	The power of belief in God and His teachings.	The power (energy) of materialism.
12.	Introspection, finding oneself.	Fatefulness of the uninitiated person.	The power of ennoblement, of equanimity, of yearning for the highest goals.	Being materially arrested, materialism, imbalance.
13.	Personal God.	Not recognizing your personal God.	The power (energy) of perfection and ennoblement.	Negative powers (energies). If not struggled against, they prevent the recognition of your personal God.
14.	General ennoblement of the spirit, the soul and the physical body through voluntary and strict asceticism.	One-sided, physical restrictions against the law for fanatical reasons.	When ascetic powers (energies) are subject to the will they control the spirit, soul, and body.	Powers that are partly or not at all controlled by a non-initiated person on all planes and in all the elements.

	Active-Positive	Passive-Negative	Active-Positive	Passive-Negative
15.	Truth.	Falsehood.	The power of the conscience.	The power of egotism or concealment.
16.	Positive attributes of the spirit in the tetrapolar magnet.	Negative attributes of the spirit in the tetrapolar magnet.	Eternal spirit, the highest principle of order of the Akasha in the astral body (Sahasrara).	The power of vibration of the tetrapolar magnet in its negative polar emanation on the mental plane.
17.	Positive attributes in the tetrapolar magnet on the astral plane.	Negative attributes in the tetrapolar magnet on the astral plane.	Soul (astral body) = seat of powers and attributes of the spirit on the astral plane.	The power of vibration of the tetrapolar magnet in its negative emanation on the astral plane.
18.	Positive attributes in the tetrapolar magnet on the material plane of a human being.	Negative attributes in the tetrapolar magnet on the material plane of a human being.	Material body with all its positive attributes. Vital powers.	The effect of the power of vibration of the tetrapolar magnet in its negative polar emanation on the material plane.
19.	The life of an initiate.	The life of a non-initiate.	Vitality in the blood and sperm (its reciprocal effect). Akasha.	Death, decomposition, the powers of the tetrapolar magnet in the principle of Earth.

B. Fire Element				
	Qualities or Attributes		Quantities or Energies	
	Active-Positive	Passive-Negative	Active-Positive	Passive-Negative
1.	Fire Element.	Fire Element.	Expansion, the ability to penetrate.	Destruction.
2.	Omnipotence.	Uncultivated will, not ennobled, normal volition.	Almighty will.	Power of the will without realization.
3.	Power of visualization, imagination, concentration.	Weak will, mediumistic tendencies.	Strengthening, condensation, preservation.	Weakening, shrinkage, obstacles.
4.	Will, volition.	Unfulfilled wishes, impulses of the will.	Controlling, creating, influencing.	Mediumistic abilities without will.

	Active-Positive	Passive-Negative	Active-Positive	Passive-Negative
5.	Electric fluid, positive.	Electric fluid, negative.	The power of emanation of the electric fluid, positive.	The power of emanation of the electric fluid, negative.
6.	Belief.	Pride.	Conviction, vitalization, realization.	Distrust, passion, skepticism.
7.	Light.	Darkness.	Penetration, condensation, the effect of the electric fluid.	Contraction, the effect of the magnetic fluid.
8.	Warmth, heat.	Winter, coldness.	Power of fire, of heat, and everything that produces warmth.	The power of water, of frost, and everything that cools.
9.	Radiation.	Darkness.	Radiating energy, electric fluid.	The power of darkness, magnetic fluid.
10.	Clairvoyance.	Normal vision on the material and astral plane.	Vitalization, improving clairvoyance.	No clairvoyance.
11.	Bravery, daring (courage).	Cowardice.	Fighting energy, the power of conviction, electric fluid.	The power of fear, of betrayal, the survival instinct.
12.	Courage, boldness.	Hesitation, evasiveness, timorousness.	Strength that leads directly to the goal without detour.	The power of fear, not trusting in oneself.
13.	Uplifting, impetus, enthusiasm, fiery.	Indifference, passitivity, aversion.	The fiery energy of ideas.	The power of antipathy and disgust.
14.	Control.	Mediumistic state, passitivity.	The power of the will.	The power of aversion.
15.	Defense, protection, aversion.	Compliance, indifference.	The power of the survival instinct.	The power of submission and compliance.
16.	Magical authority.	Imperfection, imbalance of the elements.	Omnipotence, the power of the will.	The power of the polar emanation of the negative attributes.

	Active-Positive	Passive-Negative	Active-Positive	Passive-Negative
17.	Decisiveness.	Indecision, slow to understand and think; embarrassment.	Power of perception, of the will, of intuition and inspiration.	Power of insecurity, inability to differentiate, indecisiveness.
18.	Healing.	Disturbance of the functions of the elements, illness.	The power of the electric and magnetic fluids.	Electro-magnetic fluid in an unbalanced state.
19.	Uncompromising, unyieldingness.	Willing to compromise, compliancy.	The power of conviction, of unyieldingness.	The power of intimidation, of compliance.
20.	Initiative (the spirit of enterprise).	Conservative attitude, staidness.	The power of expectation (belief) that undertakings succeed.	The power of fending off anything new and any progress.
21.	Hard on oneself.	Egotistical self-love, pampering.	The power of self-discipline.	The power of egotistical self-love, self-praise.
22.	Ennobling influence on our surroundings.	Egotistical influence on our surroundings.	Expansion in the good sense.	Expansion in an egotistical sense.
23.	Harmony.	Disharmony.	The power of love that one perceives during a sexual union.	The power of sensuality and voluptuousness perceived during a sexual union.
24.	Independence, self-sufficiency.	Dependence.	The power of independence and the best conviction.	The power of irresponsible behavior.
25.	Endurance, stability, purposefulness.	Fleetingness, moodiness, instability.	Stable and unbroken power that leads to one's goal.	The power of instability, of ill-mannered thoughts, feelings etc.
26.	Concentration.	No control over one's thoughts.	The power of the will.	The power of obstacles.
27.	Enthusiasm that is willing to sacrifice.	Egotistical enthusiasm.	The power of ennobling.	The power of thinking about one's advantages.
28.	Reliability.	Unreliability.	The power of knowledge and firm conviction.	The power of indifference and ignorance.

	Active-Positive	Passive-Negative	Active-Positive	Passive-Negative
29.	Activity.	Passivity.	The power of the electric fluid.	The power of compliance, mediumistic dependency.
30.	Equilibrium, equilibration of the elements.	Imbalance of the elements.	Power of the will.	Power of imbalanced attributes, of fate.
31.	Protection from negative influences during magical exercises.	Protection during illegal activities.	The power of seclusion in order not to be disturbed when carrying out ennobling tasks (exercises).	The power of seclusion in order not to be disturbed during illegal activities, thereby preventing their disclosure.
32.	Multifariousness.	One-sidedness.	The power of lawfulness.	The power of unlawfulness.
33.	Strong individuality.	Personal inferiority (character).	The power of the will, of the conscience.	Weak will.
34.	Successes.	Failures.	Power (strength) in overcoming obstacles.	Insufficient energy to attain success.
35.	Control of the subconscious.	Passive will, mediumistic state.	Willpower.	Powers of the negative polar emanations of the elements.
36.	The effects of a one-time important speech or lecture.	Repetition of a speech or lecture.	The power of concentration, paying attention to a good speech.	Declining attention of the listener to a speech that is repeated.
37.	Self-confidence, self-assurance.	Weak self-confidence, insecurity.	The belief in the right of one's own actions.	The power of doubt in one's own abilities and powers.
38.	Unobtrusive behavior.	Involvement in other people's affairs.	Power of respect that we show our fellowman.	The power of egotism, "I."
39.	Freshness, vitality.	Despondency, listlessness, weakness.	Active energy of the electromagnetic fluid.	Lack of energy of the electromagnetic fluid.

	Active-Positive	Passive-Negative	Active-Positive	Passive-Negative
40.	Proper asceticism.	Wish for everything that is pleasing to us.	Power of independence of all transitoriness.	The power of holding onto transitory things.
41.	Moderation.	Immoderation, voracity or gluttony (food).	The power of reason, profound innermost satisfaction, satiation of a particular element.	The power of self-indulgence, preventing the harmonious satiation of the elements.
42.	Harsh or strict on oneself.	Flattery.	The power of educating oneself.	The power of lies, hypocrisy and deceit.
43.	Humility, modesty.	Pride, powerless regret or pity.	Knowing who we are and the strength that issues from that.	Powerless energy (helplessness), arrogance.
44.	Untouchability of everything created. Everything created has its task (purpose).	Laughing at others.	The power (energy) that results from the knowledge of the significance of creation.	The power of degradation (making fun of and/or laughing at others).
45.	Modesty, simplicity.	Conceitedness, arrogance.	The power of humility.	The power of pride, of elevating oneself above others.
46.	Independence.	Being influenced by others, dependency.	The power of the will, conviction, feelings and consciousness.	The power of the mediumistic state.
47.	Magnanimity, noble-mindedness.	Stinginess.	The power of magnanimity, of unselfish help.	The power of egotism.
48.	Sensuality controlled by the will.	Uncontrolled sensuality.	The power of yearning for unification between a man and a woman.	The power of passions and eroticism.
49.	Wishing others well.	Envy.	The power of unselfish love and noble-mindedness.	The power of yearning for possessions; envious of others.

	Active-Positive	Passive-Negative	Active-Positive	Passive-Negative
50.	Indifference and not interfering in other people's personal affairs.	Jealousy.	The power of calmness and even-temperedness.	Power of wishing for something that does not belong to us.
51.	Loveliness, charm, force of attraction.	Revulsion, aversion, ugliness.	Sympathy, mutual attraction of the elements.	The power of rejection, of antipathy of the elements.
52.	Self-sacrifice, noble-mindedness.	Thirst for revenge.	The power of unselfish love, self-sacrifice.	The power of hate.
53.	Sympathy.	Hate.	Power of two interacting elements, positive.	Power of two interacting elements, negative.
54.	Peace and quiet.	Rage, annoyance.	The power of equanimity, of peace and quiet.	Power of repulsion against a situation (e.g. an insult) which is revolting, unpleasant or harmful.
55.	Modesty.	Arrogance.	Power that originates from the cognition of self-knowledge, the power of conviction.	The power of egotism.
56.	Contentment.	Irritability, tendency to unkindness, dissatisfaction, rage, explosive temper.	The power of contentment with our present situation, equanimity.	The power of everything that leads to nervous irritability and dissatisfaction.
57.	Without ambition.	Ambitious.	The power of modesty.	The power of the wish to be respected, esteemed and recognized everywhere.
58.	Having a self-confident and well thought-out plan when working.	Rash, ill-considered actions.	The power of knowledge, systematic work, skills.	The power of a fast, superficial implementation of a task. Important steps of work are not carried out.

	Active-Positive	Passive-Negative	Active-Positive	Passive-Negative
59.	Universal peace.	War, murder.	Absolute equilibrium of the elements.	The power of the highest egotism.
60.	Being fully aware of one's own imperfections.	Striving for recognition.	The power of humility.	The power of yearning for rewards and praise.
61.	Control of all (positive and negative) influences, impressions, thoughts.	Clinging to animals and their attributes.	The power of the will and cognition.	Uncontrolled power of negative influences which ties us to animals and their attributes.
62.	Determination.	Indecision.	The power of clear, sudden cognition (intuition) of what can be done in critical situations.	The power of distraction. Helplessness in critical situations and not knowing what to do.
63.	Might, power, energy of perfection and noble-mindedness.	Lack of energy.	The power of the will, omnipotence.	Weak will due to insufficiently developed Fire element.
64.	Controlling the material body.	Weakness of the organism.	The power of the will.	Weak will.
65.	Controlling the subconscious.	Insufficient control of the subconscious.	The power of the will.	Weak will.

C. Air Element			
	Qualities or Attributes		Quantities or Energies	
	Active-Positive	Passive-Negative	Active-Positive	Passive-Negative
1.	Air element, positive.	Air element, negative.	Neutralization, balance.	Destruction.
2.	Intelligence.	Egotistical "I."	Akasha Principle.	Power of egotism, of delusion.
3.	Omniscience.	Ignorance.	Akasha Principle.	The power of egotism.
4.	Knowledge, intelligence, cognition.	Primitiveness.	Intellect, reason.	The power of distrust, low level of development.

	Active-Positive	Passive-Negative	Active-Positive	Passive-Negative
5.	Consciousness.	Subconscious.	Spirit, the power of the effect of the positive attributes in the tetrapolar magnet.	Power of the effect of negative attributes in the tetrapolar magnet.
6.	Positive ideas from the causal world.	Negative ideas from causal world.	Thoughts of the positive polar emanation of the elements.	Thoughts of the negative polar emanation of the elements.
7.	Access to the events and thoughts of a previous life.	Ponderous memory when searching for past events.	Memory is the power with which we remember and are able to imagine past events. Memory is the window into the causal world.	Forgetfulness is a weak memory.
8.	We like to think about particular matters, ideas and events.	Little interest, e.g. indifferent to problems.	Perseverance when it comes to meditation and contemplation.	Instability, flightiness, negative energy that prevents us from thinking incessantly, meditation, feeling etc. for a long time.
9.	Trust.	Distrust, doubts.	The power of conviction.	Skepticism, the power of refusal.
10.	Reality, objectivity.	Lies.	Power of conviction, knowledge and proof.	Power of lies, carelessness, recklessness and ignorance.
11.	Vigilance.	Carelessness, comfortableness, indifference, compliance.	The power of self-protection.	The power of laziness, comfortableness. We do not know what we should protect ourselves from.
12.	Positive abstract concepts, ideas, secrets.	Negative abstract concepts, ideas, secrets.	The effect of the positive polar emanation of the tetrapolar magnet on thoughts.	The effect of the negative polar emanation of the tetrapolar magnet on thoughts.

	Active-Positive	Passive-Negative	Active-Positive	Passive-Negative
13.	We know the absolute truth.	Unfounded suspicion.	Power of intuition and inspiration when it comes to recognizing the absolute truth.	The power of ignorance.
14.	Joy in life.	Pessimism.	The equilibration of the elements on all planes.	Imbalance of the elements on all planes.
15.	Competence, diligence.	Laziness.	The power of positive activity.	Negative power of inactivity, loathing to work.
16.	Honesty, openness.	Dishonesty, malice.	The power of conscience and truth.	The power of egotism, lying, profit-seeking.
17.	Trust.	Distrust.	The power of belief and conviction.	The power of the selfish "I" that does not trust itself. Skepticism.
18.	Classiness, nobleness.	Conceit.	Power of humility and purity, forever in everything.	The power of arrogance.
19.	Optimism.	Pessimism.	Trust in everything positive.	Trust in everything negative.
20.	The purity of the entire creation, always and everywhere.	Differentiating between good and evil, with good being pure, and evil as impure.	The power of the absolute equilibrium of the elements, the purity of the entire creation.	The power of preventing cognition of oneself.
21.	Friendliness, friendship, sympathy.	Unfriendliness, hostility, antipathy.	The power of the mutual effects of the elements.	The power of the mutual effects of the elements.
22.	Even-tempered, balanced.	Imbalanced.	The power of the harmonious effects of the tetrapolar magnet.	Power of the disharmonious effects of the tetrapolar magnet.
23.	Perceptive faculty, astuteness.	Poor perceptive faculty, ponderousness.	The power of a mature spirit, mental matrix.	The power of an immature spirit that lags behind.
24.	Joy in life.	Pessimism.	The power of cognition that the entire creation is pure and wise.	The power of disgust against all signs of life.

	Active-Positive	Passive-Negative	Active-Positive	Passive-Negative
25.	Cheerfulness, wittiness.	Sadness, brooding.	The positive power of life's vitality that manifests in joy and harmony.	The negative power of life's tragedy, melancholy.
26.	Unobtrusiveness, non-interference.	Obtrusiveness, impertinence.	Power of modesty, of respect of one's fellowman.	The power of impertinent curiosity, exploitation.
27.	Genuine joy about the success of others.	Envy of the success of others.	The power of true love for one's fellowman.	The power of egotism.
28.	Working without praise and self-praise.	Adulation, self-praise of one's own work.	The power of modesty.	The power of an inattentive spirit.
29.	Concentrated attention. Observation of oneself and surroundings.	Inattentiveness, indifference. We pay no attention to ourselves or our surroundings.	The power of vigilance.	The power of inattentiveness.
30.	Competence.	Laziness.	Power of positive work; activity and interest in honest work.	The power of disinterest in honest work.
31.	We only wish good things for all people.	Envy, schadenfreude,[1] we wish evil things to happen to others.	The power of the universal altruism.	The power of egotistical love and envy.
32.	Cheerfulness, activity (busy).	Hesitation, slowness, minimal interest in work.	The power of willingness and liveliness of the spirit.	The power of slow perceptive faculties, minimal deployment of labor.
33.	Differentiating between something beneficial and harmful.	Ignorance, underdevelopment.	The power of introspection, of intelligence.	The power of ignorance and imbalance.
34.	Moderation.	Greed.	The power of the intellect, feelings and equanimity.	Egotistical power, deceitfulness, lack of insight.
35.	Modesty.	Exhibitionism, conceitedness.	The power of modesty.	The power of pride.

---

[1] Schadenfreude = pleasure derived from the misfortune of others. – ED.

	Active-Positive	Passive-Negative	Active-Positive	Passive-Negative
36.	Respecting the opinion of others.	Disregard for and ignoring the opinion of others.	Power of intelligence. We know that nothing in this world occurs without sense.	The power of delusion. Illusionary about one's personal "I" (ego).
37.	Carefreeness.	Excessive worries for everything transitory.	The power of conviction that Divine Providence takes care of us.	The power of clinging to everything transitory.
38.	Living in the present, in the eternal now.	Yearning for the past and curiosity about the future.	The power of the Akasha.	The power of clinging to the past and curiosity about the future.
39.	Determination.	Reaching our goal through ambition.	The power of determination.	The power of pride.
40.	Expressing ourselves correctly.	Expressing ourselves incorrectly.	The power of knowledge. The ability to express ourselves correctly.	The power of discrepancy.
41.	Caution.	Carelessness.	The power of caution when it comes to anything harmful.	The power of carelessness and slovenliness in respect to anything harmful.
42.	Proper judgment and conclusions.	False judgment and conclusions.	The power of knowledge.	The power of mistakes, of ignorance, of the subconscious.
43.	Agility, skillfulness.	Ineptness, awkwardness, clumsiness.	The power of rapid, astute comprehension.	The power of slow comprehension.
44.	Logic, logical reflection, healthy human intellect.	Illogicality, false reflection (logic).	Scientific power[2] of the connections, causes and consequences.	The power of superficiality and false knowledge.
45.	Not interfering in the affairs of others.	Interference.	Respecting the karmic laws.	Not respecting the karmic laws.
46.	Politeness.	Impolite, impertinent, and egotistical behavior.	The power of true respect and love.	The power of egotism, and a conceited "I."

---

[2] Not to be confused with man-made scientific concepts. – ED.

	Active-Positive	Passive-Negative	Active-Positive	Passive-Negative
47.	Quickness, a good sense of direction.	Ponderousness.	We immediately recognize the situation.	The power of a limited perception.
48.	We are aware of the consequences of our mistakes.	Delusion.	The power of intuition and self-cognition.	The power of ignorance.
49.	Solving problems in accordance with one's level of development.	Attempting to solve problems without success, because one is not up to or equal to the level of the problems.	The power of knowing which problems we can solve and which we cannot solve.	The power of overestimating one's own powers.
50.	We do not complain about fate, but we make the effort to eliminate the causes for our fate.	We complain about our bad fate and do not recognize that we are responsible for the causes and the consequences.	Correct assessment of causes and consequences in accordance with karmic law. The battle to eliminate negative causes.	Ignorance and blindness about the negative attributes that control a human being.
51.	We do not think about the activities of the elementaries we have created.	We disturb the elementaries when we think about them.	The power of effective help for the elementaries.	A weak will which allows the elementaries to be disturbed during their work or activities.
52.	Complete concentration on present activities.	Thoughts wander from present activity.	The power of the present, the eternal now, of concentration and the will.	The power of a weak will.
53.	We recognize the truth and admit whatever is appropriate.	We refuse to accept the truth or admit it for egotistical reasons or ignorance.	The power of conviction and the right way of dealing with matters.	The power of egotism and ignorance.
54.	We reproach no one for his mistakes, but recognize our mistakes clearly and make every effort to eliminate them.	We reproach others because of their mistakes, but do not recognize our own.	The power of a clear conscience and the cognition of the karmic laws.	The power of the ego, of ignorance, of delusion through negative attributes.

	Active-Positive	Passive-Negative	Active-Positive	Passive-Negative
55.	We do not underrate or overrate ourselves.	We overrate and underrate ourselves.	The power of self-cognition. We know what we can and cannot do.	Power of delusion, false assessment of our abilities, power of false modesty.
56.	Discretion, logical excuses, when appropriate.	Egotistical lies, excuses covering up mistakes or crimes.	The power of discretion. We never disclose secrets to non-initiates.	Power of angst and refusal to admit certain mistakes and make changes for the better.
57.	General interest in the entire creation.	Interest in matters that are beneficial for egotistical reasons.	The power of knowledge of the universal laws of creation.	Power of lack of knowledge of the universal laws of creation. Power of ignorance and egotism.
58.	Well thought-out conclusions, agreeing at the right time.	Ill-considered proposals and objections without considering and understanding the subject.	The power of a developed and mature intellect.	The power of disharmony in the intellect.
59.	Freshness.	Weakness, listlessness.	Power of youth. Developing the elements in harmony.	The malfunction of the emanation of an element.
60.	Clear cognition.	Limited cognition in accordance with the level of development and maturity.	High level of intelligence.	Imperfection of the Air element that expresses itself in a lack of recognition and the ability to differentiate.
61.	Justified caution.	Carelessness and egotistical (selfish) caution.	Power that warns us about anything harmful and which would obstruct our progress.	We are careless and do not maintain the equilibrium of the elements.
62.	Eternal youth.	Ageing.	The power of the perfect tetrapolar magnet and the cognition of who we really are.	Power of the negative Earth element that decomposes the body, soul, and the immature spirit.

	Active-Positive	Passive-Negative	Active-Positive	Passive-Negative
63.	Genuine, multifarious progress.	One-sided progress.	The power of knowledge, of universal intelligence.	The power of limited development in only one aspect.
64.	Freedom.	Slavery, being inferior, being at the mercy of particular powers, attributes and influences.	Basic equilibrium on all planes, the power of adaptation.	The negatively influencing power of the unbalanced tetrapolar magnet on all planes.
65.	Multifariousness, individuality.	Limitedness, commonness.	Yearning for cognition and differentiation from the point of view of our own self-cognition.	The power of mass development. Personal development that depends on the whole.
66.	Complete tranquility, equanimity, serenity.	Curiosity.	Complete equilibrium of the elements.	Yearning to find out what is none of our concern.
67.	Cleanliness and purity, always and in all things.	Uncleanliness and impurity.	The power of perfection, of ennoblement.	Negative attributes that control a human being.
68.	Courage, daring (Fire element).	Fear of death etc.	The power of the will, of belief and conviction.	Survival instinct (urge for self-preservation), fear through ignorance of the unknown worlds of the higher spheres.
69.	Overcoming obstacles. Fortifying the spirit, the soul and the physical body.	Resignation without a battle because of laziness, weakness, and cowardice.	Practice to overcome obstacles when doing our exercises.	The power of the unbalanced elements.
70.	Discreetness, silence.	Disclosing secrets.	The power of not revealing secrets.	The power of talkativeness, the urge to talk, the weakness of uncontrollable talking.
71.	We attach our thoughts to the "now" (present only).	Return of senseless thoughts.	Power of the present, of eternity, e.g. no time, no space.	The power that draws us into the past, fixating on transitory things.

	Active-Positive	Passive-Negative	Active-Positive	Passive-Negative
72.	Interest in significant and enormous events, problems, causes, reasons and consequences.	Pettiness, superficiality, the lack of ability to overcome matters of the soul.	The power of the mature and developed spirit.	The power of the underdeveloped and immature spirit.
73.	Modesty, discreetness.	The desire to impress.	Power of humility, of discretion.	The power of pride.
74.	Do no exaggerate facts.	Distorting facts.	The power of truth.	The power of lies, of fantasy.
75.	We express ourselves clearly and distinctly, and adhere to the truth.	Verbal incompetence.	Verbal competence.	Verbal incompetence.
76.	Proper assessment.	Naivety, childishness.	The power of knowledge.	The power of childlike trust.
77.	Adhering to the facts and realizing what is essential.	Flattery.	The cognition of what is essential, and what is truth.	The power of the deliberate embellishment for egotistical (selfish) reasons.
78.	Calmness, perfection, ennoblement.	Imbalance in one's character.	Power of a balanced character.	General weakness.
79.	Proper assessment.	Exaggeration, overstatement.	The power of cognition.	The power of false assessment.
80.	Levelheadedness, circumspection.	Thoughtlessness.	The power of good sense, of intelligence and reason.	Acting rashly and impulsively and the consequences.
81.	Reason.	Unreasonableness.	Healthy and sound human intellect.	The power of a weakly developed intellect.
82.	Proceeding slowly but cautiously.	Acting rashly and impulsively.	The power of systematics, and proceeding in a thorough and well thought-out way.	The wish to reach our goal immediately.
83.	We are conscious of ourselves.	Absent-mindedness, scattered thoughts, unable to focus.	The power that controls our senses and thoughts and directs them to our present activities.	The power of distraction with our present activities.

	Active-Positive	Passive-Negative	Active-Positive	Passive-Negative
84.	Good-naturedness, honesty.	Maliciousness.	The power of true love for the entire creation.	The power of an evil will.
85.	Good, solid, honest work and occupation.	Carelessness at work and all activities.	The power of improving our conscientiousness.	Indifferent attitude toward work and all our activities.
86.	Calmness, concentration.	Absent-mindedness.	The power of a well-balanced temperament (the tetrapolar magnet).	Power of subordinate thoughts.
87.	We respect all people the way they are.	We laugh and make fun of other people.	The power of acting properly and the right attitude toward creation.	By laughing at other people, we make ourselves look ridiculous and ugly.
88.	Not interfering in other people's business.	Demanding, interfering in other people's private lives, goading people into doing something.	Do not encroach on other people's territory.	The power of provocation, instigating people to commit evil deeds.
89.	Punctuality, meticulousness, consequence.	Apologies, excuses for slovenliness, and sloppy work.	We keep our word and we fulfill our duties.	We do not keep our word or our resolutions, and we do not fulfill our duties and obligations.
90.	We are attentive.	Inattentiveness.	Cognizant power.	Immaturity. We do not recognize the nature of things.
91.	Discernment, good ability to judge.	Prejudicial and rash decision-making.	The power of knowledge, intuition, inspiration.	The power of immaturity and ignorance of the nature of things.
92.	Stability, permanence.	Changeable and unstable character.	The power of perseverance and stability, willpower.	The power of an erratic and uncontrolled spirit.
93.	Firm and unshakable convictions.	Fickleness.	Active power or energy.	The power of fickleness, inability to differentiate between right or wrong.

	Active-Positive	Passive-Negative	Active-Positive	Passive-Negative
94.	Skill, nimbleness.	Ineptness.	Power or energy through mental exercises.	Power of insufficient practice of one's mental exercises, powers in a raw state.
95.	Logical thinking.	Illogicality.	Results of correct reflections and conclusions.	The power of illogicality, gaps in and lack of logic.
96.	True love for one's fellowman, which expresses itself in helpfulness.	Exploitation.	The power of true love and harmony.	We are attached to wealth and material things.
97.	Honoring and revering old age.	Cursing old age.	The power of the elements (Earth) that decompose the physical and astral bodies.	All blame is put on old age.
98.	Not interfering in matters that are none of our business.	Interfering in other people's matters or affairs.	The power of not interfering in another's fate.	The consequences of acting against the karmic laws.
99.	Behavior or conduct that does not arouse or irritate the negative attributes of our fellowman.	Behavior or conduct that arouses or irritates the negative attributes of our fellowman.	The power of equanimity and ennoblement.	The power of egotism.
100.	Complete thought concentration with our present activities.	Scattered and roaming thoughts, and inattentiveness.	The power of the will and conviction.	The power of an untrained spirit, the power of the subconscious, weak will.
101.	We act from our own point of view voluntarily.	Slavish mannerism, servitude, submissiveness.	The power of independence.	The power of dependence.
102.	Modesty and honest joy about the success of others.	Ambition, wanting always to be first.	The power of respect about the positive attributes of others.	The power of ambition and fear to be professionally degraded.
103.	Neutral, external appearance, we adaptability.	Special attention to a pretty external appearance; we want to be liked by everyone.	Inconspicuousness, decency, proper appearance.	The power of smugness, of a lavish appearance.

	Active-Positive	Passive-Negative	Active-Positive	Passive-Negative
104.	Calm and composed behavior toward our fellowman.	We cannot bear to be watched, observed or stared at.	Basic equilibrium.	Imbalance. We cannot bear to be observed by others.
105.	Discreetness, reticence.	Talkativeness, we cannot keep anything to ourselves.	The power of reticence.	Power of boasting and talkativeness. We disclose what others should not know.
106.	We see our mistakes and consequences clearly and we control them.	We play down or minimize our mistakes and their consequences, and we slacken our fight against them.	Vigilance toward all negative attributes.	The power of disguising our negative attributes.
107.	Good behavior, good manners.	Bad behavior and manners, e.g. we interrupt another person when he or she is speaking.	The power of politeness.	The power of the egotistical and conceited "I."
108.	Well thought-out activities.	Carelessness.	The power of a healthy intellect.	Power of unreasonableness (stupidity), thoughtlessness and irresponsibility.
109.	Unselfish help.	We demand rewards for good deeds.	The power of ennoblement and love.	The power of egotism and ambition.
110.	Consciousness, control.	Stupidity, wickedness.	Power of the normal consciousness.	The power of the subconscious.
111.	Comprehension, the ability to assess any situation. Secrets we can assess and which we are able to handle astrally.	Unsuccessful and senseless attempts to understand secrets; to comprehend situations that surpass our psychic (astral) powers.	The power of intuition, of self-cognition.	To recognize our inability to comprehend a matter because it is beyond our abilities.
112.	We understand the causal law of cause, effect and consequence and make the effort to eliminate the negative causes.	The battle against destiny.	The power of introspection.	The power of ignorance and delusion.

	Active-Positive	Passive-Negative	Active-Positive	Passive-Negative
113.	We leave elementals in peace by not thinking about them.	We disturb the elementals during their work by thinking about them.	The power of peace and quiet; we do not disturb other beings while they work.	We disturb other beings without a good reason while they work.
114.	We must always completely focus on the matter at hand.	Uncontrolled thoughts.	The power of the consciousness.	The power of the subconscious.
115.	We talk our way out of something for good reasons.	We talk our way out of something without good reasons.	The power of reticence.	The power of lies and egotism.
116.	We disclose as much truth as an uninitiated person is permitted to know in accordance with his maturity.	We deny the truth for egotistical reasons.	The power of the lawfulness of truth.	The power of unlawfulness, of lies.
117.	We know the truth and live accordingly.	We admit everything that is pleasant, but conceal the unpleasant mistakes.	The power of lawfulness and honesty.	The power of egotism and unlawfulness, of delusion.
118.	We do not judge other people.	We criticize other people, but we are not approachable to any kind of criticism.	Knowledge and control of the law of karma.	The power of egotism, of ignorance and not being in control of the law of karma.
119.	Courteous behavior. We have respect for the abilities of others.	We only respect ourselves.	The power of basic equilibrium.	The power of selfishness and imbalance.

D. Water Element			
Qualities or Attributes		Quantities or Energies	
Active-Positive	Passive-Negative	Active-Positive	Passive-Negative
1. Good will, ennoblement.	Evil will.	The power of help where karma allows it.	The power of egotism and hate.

	Active-Positive	Passive-Negative	Active-Positive	Passive-Negative
2.	Honesty, directness.	Dishonesty, cunningness.	The power of truth and truth in others.	The power of dishonesty and cunningness.
3.	Sympathy, love.	Antipathy, hate.	Power of genuine help, of the reciprocal effects of the elements.	The power of hate, of the reciprocal effects of the elements.
4.	Indifference to false compassion and curiosity etc.	Curious about everything that is none of our business.	We know the effects of negative attributes (characteristics).	The power of curiosity.
5.	Modesty, humility.	Immodesty, pride.	We are aware of our own value; we neither underrate nor overrate ourselves.	A yearning for everything we do not possess and do not deserve. Conceitedness, exaggerated opinion of ourselves.
6.	Tranquility.	Unrest, nervousness, scatterbrained.	Equanimity, always and everywhere.	Imbalance of the elements, especially in our conscience and subconscious.
7.	We offend no one.	Offensiveness.	Power of equanimity, e.g., nothing can offend us.	We retreat because we are easily offended.
8.	Respect for our fellowman.	No respect for others.	The power of true love and respect, which we extend to the immortal spirit of others.	The power of the selfish "I," which respects only itself and everything that provides it with an advantage.
9.	Honesty.	Dishonesty.	The power of conviction to do everything within our power to ennoble our spirit, our soul and our physical body.	The power to exploit other people, of egotism and thinking of gaining an advantage.
10.	Contentment, blissfulness.	Discontentment, dissatisfaction.	The power of a clear conscience.	Power of all mistakes and errors which were not settled through positive actions.

	Active-Positive	Passive-Negative	Active-Positive	Passive-Negative
11.	The will controls feelings.	Feelings control the will.	Power of the will that controls and rules feelings.	A weak will which is controlled by feelings.
12.	We are tolerant and kind to other people whenever necessary.	Very strict toward other people, but tolerant with ourselves.	The power of politeness.	The power of the egotistical "I."
13.	Health.	Illness.	The vital energy of universal health and equilibrium of the elements.	The power of imbalanced elements in a human being.
14.	Fertility, belief.	Infertility.	The power of astral fertility, of manifested belief.	Power of impeding astral fertility, and skepticism.
15.	Active life, rhythm, movement, optimism.	Negation of life, pessimism, hardening, irregularity.	The power of the conscious tetrapolar magnet.	The power of the tetrapolar magnet effective in the subconscious.
16.	Cold-bloodedness, coldness.	Hot-bloodedness, heat.	The coldness of the Water element.	The uncontrolled power of heat, the expansive power of the Fire element.
17.	Kindness.	Rude behavior.	The power of politeness.	The power of rudeness, of naughtiness, of egotism.
18.	Patience.	Impatience.	The power of endurance in overcoming obstacles.	The power of impatience, the fleetingness that prevents us from developing the endurance to overcome obstacles.
19.	Mercy.	Emotional frigidity, cruelty.	The power of true love and helpfulness.	The power of egotism.
20.	Justified willingness to sacrifice.	Refusing any kind of sacrifice.	Power of conviction that all things belong to Providence. We sacrifice ourselves for others, if they deserve it.	We only think about our own advantages, egotism.

	Active-Positive	Passive-Negative	Active-Positive	Passive-Negative
21.	We yearn for the highest goal.	We only yearn for lowest goals of the egotistical "I."	The power of attraction of the highest perfection, ennoblement.	The power of attraction of the material plane.
22.	Forgiveness.	We cannot and will not forgive.	The conviction that everything that was done to us by others is a matter of our destiny. We forgive gladly.	The power of hate and being offended. We do not accept any apology; we do not accept any reason to forgive.
23.	Gratitude.	Ingratitude.	We value what other people have done for us.	We forget all the good things that have been done for us and repay good with evil.
24.	Well-founded obedience.	Unfounded obedience.	The power of conscience.	The power that does not pay attention to the conscience.
25.	The appropriate attitude to things that got lost.	Misusing occult power to find lost things.	The power of the law. Not using occult powers for common things.	Misuse of occult powers for profane things.
26.	The proper attitude toward the departed.	Mourning over and being unable to forget the departed.	The power of conviction that we must forget those who have died, so that we do not disturb them in the astral or mental worlds.	The power of creating phantoms that nourish themselves from the astral energy of their creator; vampirism.
27.	Self-criticism.	Criticizing others.	The power of ennobling the human character.	Using one's will to interfere with the karma of others.
28.	We do not complain; instead we help ourselves.	We weep over our fate and mishaps.	We recognize the karmic law which forgives all deeds.	We make others responsible for our fate and demand help from them.
29.	Reality, truth, knowledge, intelligence.	Illusion, lies, distorting facts, imagination running wild.	The power of cognition of the absolute truth.	Power of ignorance, a weak will, giving in; negative mediumistic state.

	Active-Positive	Passive-Negative	Active-Positive	Passive-Negative
30.	We reject the wish for success.	We yearn for successes when developing our magical powers.	The power of yearning for the ennobling of the spirit, soul and physical body.	Egotistical power that demands what it does not deserve.
31.	In awe of God.	Not in awe of God.	The power of cognition of our nothingness in comparison to God.	The power of disregard or contempt of the universal laws.
32.	Courage, willingness to take a risk, daring.	Cowardice, shyness.	The power of self-confidence.	The power of timidity (fearfulness) and weakness when we possess no self-confidence.
33.	Justified appeal for help.	Unjustified demands to get help.	The power of justified help for everyone.	The power of seduction for egotistical reasons to demand help which would intervene with destiny.
34.	Impartiality.	Prejudice, partiality.	The power that protects us from prejudice (partiality); neutral and objective attitude, impartiality.	The power of clinging to one thing, one-sidedness.
35.	Indifference where it is appropriate.	Indifference when you really should help.	The power of indifference toward the negative activities of other beings.	The power of heartlessness, insensitivity in situations where we should help.
36.	Appropriate attitude toward negative attributes.	We are not aware that we are influenced by negative characteristics (attributes).	We recognize our negative attributes and have them under our control.	The power of negative attributes that control human beings.
37.	Mindfulness, carefulness.	Indifference.	The power of interest in life, in work etc.	The power of indifference; negative outlook on life and work.

	Active-Positive	Passive-Negative	Active-Positive	Passive-Negative
38.	Imperturbability.	Compliance (giving-in).	The power of belief and will.	The power of lack of independence.
39.	Admit mistakes, modesty.	Defiance, inflexibility, obstinacy.	The power of cognition.	The power of incomprehensibility and defiance.
40.	Activity, determination (also Fire element).	Passivity.	The power of the will, positive activity.	The power of weak nerves.
41.	Polite behavior.	Primitive behavior, animalistic plane.	The power of respect toward other people.	The power of naughtiness; no respect for others.
42.	Moderation.	Exaggerated enthusiasm or fending off (e.g. fans.)	The will controls feelings.	Feelings control the will.
43.	You are aware of the higher planes and their inhabitants.	Fetishism. Worshipping the departed.	You respect that a person after leaving the material world has peace in order to develop further on the astral and mental planes.	Exaggerated, uncontrollable and extremely developed love toward departed people and clinging to them.
44.	Unshakable attitude.	Losing one's composure.	The power of clear knowledge, the ability to decide, and conviction.	The power of negative attributes that cannot be overcome because a weak will.
45.	Complete control of feelings in critical moments.	Overly sensitive.	The power to control all expression of feelings.	The power of feelings which are not controlled by the will.
46.	Multifariousness, universality.	Partiality.	Complete harmony of the tetrapolar magnet.	The power of onesidedness (partiality) which is effective in only one direction, while all other directions in one's development are ignored.
47.	Absolute truth, wisdom.	Relative and subjective personal truth.	Complete self-cognition, knowledge and command of the universal laws.	The power of relativity, incomplete subjective cognition.

	Active-Positive	Passive-Negative	Active-Positive	Passive-Negative
48.	Openness when appropriate.	Being evasive when it is not appropriate.	The power of truth, at any price.	The power of dishonesty; we do not admit your mistakes.
49.	The ability to differentiate.	We accept everything without thinking about it, without conviction, without understanding.	The power of cognition and being in command of the universal laws.	The power of superficiality, of wickedness, irresponsibility and carelessness.
50.	The appropriate willingness to sacrifice.	Willing to sacrifice without reflection.	The power of true love and help.	Blind power that helps those who do not deserve help because of karmic burdens.
51.	Independence.	We are influenced by human beings and beings.	The power of individuality.	An undesirable mediumistic state.
52.	Criticism during self-cognition.	Criticism from a subjective point of view.	The power of introspection.	The power of the subjective "I" that rejects everything that appears to be harmful from an egotistical point of view.
53.	Self-cognition, introspection.	Exaggerated moral feelings.	The power that leads a human being to perfection.	Uncontrollable feelings; we give everything an emotional bias.
54.	Sincere yearning for truth and fondness for reality.	Detesting the truth; fondness for unreality and lies.	The power of truth always and everywhere.	The power of lies and distorting facts in our fantasy.
55.	Harsh and strict toward oneself.	Turning soft, pampering.	The power of proper upbringing and the ability to resist.	The power of weakness and giving in (compliance).
56.	Independence. Control over our thoughts and the expressions or remarks of beings that want to force themselves on us (subconscious).	We react to thoughts and expressions or remarks of beings that force themselves on us (subconscious).	The power of the will, of control (Fire).	The power of a weak will, not being in control. Mediumistic state.

	Active-Positive	Passive-Negative	Active-Positive	Passive-Negative
57.	Feelings controlled by the will.	Stirred-up emotional feelings on various occasions.	The power of the will (Fire).	Feelings that control the will; uncontrolled emotional life.
58.	Genuine reality.	Deceit in a fantastical state, deceit in a utopian state, deception, swindle.	The power of the universal truth and the universal laws.	The power of unreality, of deception; we do not recognize the universal laws and the truth.
59.	True yearning for love and love for God.	Detesting or loathing God.	The power of true love for God leading to self-cognition.	Not knowing oneself, loathing oneself and loathing or detesting God.
60.	Reality.	Distorted half-truths.	The power of reality, the path to the truth.	The power of detesting the truth and removing ourselves from reality and truth.
61.	Independence (Fire element).	Imitating or emulating other people.	The power of cognition and the will.	The power of dependency, fondness of comfort, and slavery.
62.	Lack of ambition.	Ambition. Wishes fulfilled in accordance with dignity and distinction (reputation, rank, academic degrees, entitlement etc.).	The power of modesty.	The power of immodesty, of ambition, and striving for promotions.
63.	Normal consciousness.	Artificially produced emotional states, moods, above all those which are pleasant and induce sleep.	The positive power of the tetrapolar magnet.	The negative power of the Water element that calls forth undesired and uncontrolled emotional states, moods etc.
64.	Yearning for ennobling the spirit, the soul and the physical body in the tetrapolar magnet.	Yearning for successes.	The power of recognizing who we are.	The negative power which binds a person for egotistical reasons to the material plane.

	Active-Positive	Passive-Negative	Active-Positive	Passive-Negative
65.	Permanent equilibrium of the elements.	Underrating ourselves.	The power of equanimity and proper assessment of one's own abilities and skills.	The power of ignorance and weakness, lacking self-confidence.
66.	Eternal now — the present.	Longing for the past or the future.	The power of the Akasha principle.	The power that binds a person to the material plane.
67.	Indifference toward the mistakes of other people and keeping silent about their bad attributes.	Schadenfreude. Displaying a gloating behavior at the mistakes of others.	The power of respecting the laws of karma which are in effect everywhere.	The power of schadenfreude and disrespecting the karmic laws. We accuse other people of their mistakes.
68.	Complete self-control.	Lack of certainty.	The power of proper self-assessment.	The power of uncertain and false self-assessment.
69.	Certainty in accordance with our own level of development.	Lack of certainty.	The power of proper self-assessment.	The power of uncertain and false self-assessment.
70.	Awe of God.	No respect for God.	The power of true love and humility for God.	The power of delusion and pride.
71.	We work by ourselves on ourselves and do not rely on the help of others leading to self-contentedness.	We demand help in cases where it is not necessary.	The power of independence, self-contentedness when building the perfect and ennobled temple of Solomon.	We rely on other people's help, the power of dependency and lack of self-contentedness.
72.	We are taciturn, practicing silence when it comes to uninitiated people.	We use our abilities to impress other people.	The power of secrets (mysteries) and silence.	The power that misuses occult abilities to perform them in front of uninitiated people.
73.	Absolute equilibrium of the elements.	Melancholy, pessimism.	The power of the tetrapolar magnet, completely balanced on all planes.	Negative power of melancholy, hopelessness, mourning, pessimism (Water element).

	Active-Positive	Passive-Negative	Active-Positive	Passive-Negative
74.	Élan, joy of life, vitality, sparkle with life, youthful fire.	Depression, sadness, weakness, despondency, lack of energy, exhaustion.	The power of the positive attributes of the Fire and Air elements.	The power of depression, of exhausted nerves.
75.	Strict control of all impressions, of sensory perceptions, thoughts, feelings, the ability to distinguish.	The possibility exists that we are constantly being cheated and deceived.	The power of introspection and universal truth.	The power of uncontrolled and unsorted thoughts, impressions and concepts.
76.	The belief in all lawfulness and truth.	Lack of faith.	Power of belief; conviction of truth and lawfulness.	The power of mistrust, of skepticism.
77.	Having the will and courage to realize and have our justifiable wishes and those of our fellowman come true.	The will and courage do not suffice to realize wishes.	The power of the will and conviction that we can achieve anything we wish.	The power of doubt that we can achieve our wishes.
78.	Realistic point of view, assessment of how much we can achieve.	Fantastical dreams of success without work.	The power of truth, knowledge and lawfulness.	The power of lies, of deception, concepts and illusions.
79.	Recognition and having command of the universal laws.	Lack of clarity, uncertainty.	The power of knowledge and control of the universal laws.	The power of lack of knowledge (ignorance) of the universal laws.
80.	Impartiality, objectivity, universal attitude, position and viewpoint.	Prejudice, partiality.	The power of cognition of the true "I" (spirit).	The power of a one-sided character.
81.	Hard on oneself; we conceal every kind of pain, any unpleasantness and any suffering.	We yearn for compassion, and have pity on oneself.	We know we should bear pleasant things and unpleasant things with patience and joy.	Power of egotism. We want to rid ourselves of suffering through the compassion of other people.
82.	Courage, fearlessness.	Fearfulness, cowardice, shyness.	Power of the will, belief, conviction, cognition.	Power of fear, the urge and desire for self-preservation.

	Active-Positive	Passive-Negative	Active-Positive	Passive-Negative
83.	Fearlessness, openness, joy of life.	Timidity.	Joy of living, optimism.	The power of exaggerated worries, of pessimism.
84.	We reject low-level goals.	We react to material and low goals.	We recognize and control all our negative characteristics that are active within us.	We tolerate the effects of negative attributes and are guided by them.
85.	Silence, discreetness.	Confiding in someone naïvely, gullibility.	The power and might of silence.	We do not possess insight into human nature. Carelessness.
86.	We value our own powers, attributes and abilities properly.	We underrate ourselves.	The power of belief.	Lack of belief in ourselves.
87.	Correct assessment of our negative attributes.	Incorrect assessment of our negative attributes.	The power of self-cognition, of introspection.	The power of ignorance, of delusion.
88.	Patience.	Impatience.	Conviction that with patience, despite temporary failures, we will reach our goal.	Power of impatience, of distrust. We want to reach a goal quickly, without perseverance.
89.	The correct assessment of one's own mistakes.	Exaggerated self-reproach, self-accusation.	The power of the equilibrium of the elements and true introspection.	Power that underestimates one's development, personal value, and state (tetrapolar magnet).
90.	Determining one's own matters of fate and that of other people.	Annoyances and worries (problems) about the loss of a possession or a loved one (living being).	The power of cognition and command of the karmic laws.	The power of ignorance and uncontrollability of the karmic laws.
91.	We never speak about something that is of no interest those we are speaking to.	We empathically and deliberately repeat topics which no one is interested in.	We are aware of the interests of others and we adjust to or accommodate their character, request or concern.	We force our opinion, our own points of view on others, which are of no interest and which are repulsive.

	Active-Positive	Passive-Negative	Active-Positive	Passive-Negative
92.	We do not cling to anything transitory.	We cling to music and other transitory things.	The power of the development of the immortal spirit to the highest goals.	The power of attraction to the material plane; immaturity of the spirit.
93.	We are independent of foreign influences.	Influenced by the beings of the invisible world.	The power of the will and independence.	The power of dependency on all things, on attributes, and on a mediumistic state.
94.	Honest, genuine joy.	False, pretended joy.	The power of optimism, of an open character.	Power of dishonesty that shows itself in false joy.
95.	We have insight into our own mistakes and we make the effort to eliminate them.	We are annoyed at our own mistakes.	The power of introspection and conscience.	The power that shackles us to our mistakes which we do not consider to be an incentive for change.
96.	Vigilance, attentiveness. Only relying on one's own judgment.	Apathy — we rely on Providence.	The power of development, of protection and the defense of the eternal spirit.	The power of passivity, of inability, indifference and ignorance of one's own attributes and abilities on which we should rely on at all times.
97.	Moderate, natural, normal conditions guided by one's own will.	Unnatural, unwanted conditions.	The power of the all-controlling will.	The power of negative influences, unwanted negative and active attributes.
98.	Peace.	War: Egotism, hateful, envious, vengeful, destructive state of affairs (Fire element).	The activities of the balanced tetrapolar magnet (Water element).	The actions of the power of the unbalanced tetrapolar magnet (Fire element).
99.	Hope.	Skepticism, distrust.	Partial trust in success.	Complete distrust of being successful.
100.	We unconditionally keep our word and promise.	We do not keep our word.	The power of the highest virtue, of a promise.	We do not see ourselves as a spirit created in God's image.

	E. Earth Element				
	Qualities or Attributes		Quantities or Energies	
	Active-Positive	Passive-Negative	Active-Positive	Passive-Negative
1.	We do not cling to anything transitory.	We cling to material things, wealth, good food etc.	We are aware that nothing really belongs to us — we are merely stewards.	The power of the force of attraction toward the material.
2.	Proper assessment of oneself with the help of introspection.	False assessment of oneself.	The power of proper introspection, self-cognition, the knowledge of one's own powers, attributes and abilities.	The power of one's own overestimation or underestimation without introspection.
3.	Equanimity, balance.	Imbalance.	The power of the equilibrium of the elements.	The power that is effective in the unbalanced tetrapolar magnet.
4.	Well thought-out and calm handling of how we proceed with our work and other activity.	We are scatter-brained and lack concentration.	The power of concentration and attentiveness in all activities.	The power of lack of concentration and carelessness in all activities.
5.	We use our power only for thoughts, feelings and deeds that are useful or beneficial.	We squander our power by doing something senseless and harmful.	The power of cognition, of how to use our power properly.	Dealing in an ignorant and unsystematic manner with our powers.
6.	We learn from experience.	We have not learned from experience.	The power of wisdom.	The power of carelessness.
7.	Justice, justness.	Injustice.	The power of lawfulness.	The power of unlawfulness.
8.	We respect other people's property.	We use, misuse, destroy, and misappropriate things that are not ours.	We should not touch something that does not belong to us.	The power by which you acquire the possessions of other people.

	Active-Positive	Passive-Negative	Active-Positive	Passive-Negative
9.	Correct contemplation or thinking, judgments that correspond with truth.	Thinking or contemplation and judgments that do not correspond with truth.	The power of truth.	The power of unreality.
10.	We make an effort to educate ourselves which leads to introspection.	Education and upbringing is left solely to karma. No personal input.	The power of self-education. Self-cognition.	The power of fateful causes and the consequences thereof.
11.	Moderation, always and everywhere.	Immoderation.	Intuitive limit regarding the quantities of everything we take in.	The power of insatiability. Not in possession of the appropriate or adequate feelings when satiated, e.g. no boundaries.
12.	We respect other people the way they are.	We do not respect other people the way they are.	The power of knowledge and of controlling the karmic laws.	The power of ignorance and having no command of the karmic laws.
13.	We keep our word, promises, and vows.	We do not keep our word, promises, and vows.	The power of an unconditional commitment and the honor of the eternal spirit.	The power of fraud and loss of honor.
14.	Asceticism.	An undisciplined and convenient life.	The power of strictness toward oneself, of self-education.	The power of fateful consequences that a human being harvests for negative causes.
15.	Punctuality, always and everywhere.	Lack of punctuality, inaccuracy.	The power of discipline, of obedience, of intention and duty.	Power of lack of discipline, of disobedience, of not respecting duty and intention.
16.	Imperturbability, a hard life, strict on oneself.	Frailty, doubt, carelessness, self-love.	The power of the will, of conviction, asceticism.	A weak will, inclination to a comfortable life, to wealth, to the pursuit of desires and pleasures.

	Active-Positive	Passive-Negative	Active-Positive	Passive-Negative
17.	Stable character.	Instability, moodiness.	The power of endurance and conviction.	The power of changing moods and an undeveloped intellect.
18.	Consciousness.	Subconscious.	Intellect – the effectiveness of the positive attributes in the tetrapolar magnet.	Intellect – the effectiveness of the negative attributes in the tetrapolar magnet.
19.	Agreeableness, tolerance.	Incompatibility, intolerance.	Power of harmony and acceptance of points of view and manners of thinking of other people at their level of development.	The power of disharmony, lack of respect, interference with and suppression of the opinions of others.
20.	Sobriety, always and everywhere.	Excess.	The power of the intuitive feelings of satiation.	The power of insatiability.
21.	Systematics.	Breakdown, disorder.	You keep the matter at hand in the appropriate order.	The power of illogical procedures pertaining to work and other activities.
22.	Good deeds.	Evil deeds.	The power of ennoblement.	The power of egotism.
23.	Objectivity, universal attitude.	Subjectivity, biased attitude.	The power of knowledge of the universal laws and analogies.	The power of lack of knowledge (ignorance) of the universal laws and analogies, of one-sidedness.
24.	Silence, discreetness.	Profanity. Disclosure of secrets.	The power of silence.	The power of profanity and the disclosure of secrets.
25.	Thriftiness, accumulation.	Squandering of possessions in any manner and extravagance.	The power that maintains energy reserves within us.	The power of carelessness and the senseless extravagance of our powers and abilities.

	Active-Positive	Passive-Negative	Active-Positive	Passive-Negative
26.	We make the effort to use everything for its true best.	Dealing irresponsibly with the means that are given to us, without any consideration as to whether the intentions are good or evil.	The power of ennoblement.	The power of irresponsibility, of indifference.
27.	Reality.	Lies, fantasy, unreality.	The power of lawfulness and truth.	The power of unlawfulness.
28.	Harmony.	Disharmony.	The power of the effectiveness of a perfectly balanced tetrapolar magnet.	The power of an imbalanced tetrapolar magnet.
29.	Strict on oneself, even at an old age.	Sinning against the elderly.	The power of the eternal spirit.	Weakness of the spirit, which is subject to the natural decline of the physical body.
30.	We take good care of our external appearance.	Carelessness on the material plane.	The power of asceticism on the material plane.	The power of imbalance on the material plane in regards to the external.
31.	We take every situation seriously and judge it correctly in accordance with its significance and the nature of things.	We are careless with matters that concern us.	The power of cognition and differentiation in every situation that comes our way.	The power of carelessness in matters which we erroneously consider unimportant.
32.	Intelligence, improving the character.	We make no effort to increase our intelligence and improve our character.	The power of knowledge, of wisdom, and yearning for perfection.	Power of carelessness, indifference in contrast to self-cognition and ennoblement of oneself.
33.	The correct assessment of our mistakes.	We do not acknowledge our mistakes.	Power of conscience, of intuition and introspection.	Power of delusion through negative attributes that we do not want to acknowledge.

	Active-Positive	Passive-Negative	Active-Positive	Passive-Negative
34.	We do not condemn others or speak badly of them.	We condemn other people and speak badly about them.	The power of knowledge and being in command of the karmic laws.	Negative power of ignorance of the karmic laws and oneself.
35.	Appropriate care of earthly possessions to which we do not cling.	We occupy ourselves and care excessively for material things to which we are attached.	Well-balanced relationship of our present life to other planes.	Excessively attached to material things.
36.	Good habits.	Bad, harmful habits.	Power of good habits. The ability to distinguish what harms us and what helps us.	The power of negative habits which we are not conscious of.
37.	Enthusiasm for exercises that ennoble our spirit, soul and physical body.	Listlessness, aversion to exercises with the goal to ennoble ourselves.	The power of ennoblement and perfection that attract and shape a human being.	The power of imperfection and immaturity to ennoble ourselves.
38.	Preparedness to help, to do something noble, even if self-sacrifice is involved.	We are not prepared to help people in need or do something noble.	The power of true love and noble-mindedness.	The power of egotism that prevents a human being from doing something noble.
39.	Unselfishness.	Selfishness, thinking about our own advantage, profit-seeking.	The power of true noble-mindedness and love for our fellowman, renouncing cherished possessions for the benefit of others.	The power of egotism, of greed and profiteering.
40.	Proper orientation.	False orientation.	The power of fast recognition and of discernment in all situations.	The power of ignorance that seduces us to take the wrong path.
41.	Generosity.	Stinginess.	The power of love and best wishes for our fellowman which reveals itself through generosity.	The power of cruel egotism and an obsession with mammonism; we only see ourselves.

	Active-Positive	Passive-Negative	Active-Positive	Passive-Negative
42.	We do not react to the worthless remarks of other people.	We react to the worthless remarks of other people, and we abide by them thereby harming ourselves.	The power of independence and being conscious of our own true being.	The power of attraction to the sphere of negative attributes which takes the necessary astral powers from us.
43.	We do not underestimate ourselves or other human beings.	We underestimate ourselves and other people.	The power of far-sightedness, of modesty and trust.	We have no trust or confidence in ourselves or others.
44.	We continue faithfully with the exercises and instructions regarding our magical development.	We do not follow through with the exercises and instructions on magical development.	The power of perseverance and yearning for the highest goal.	Power of egotism that leads us astray from our highest goal to lesser successes, e.g., we develop magical power to misuse them.
45.	Genuine universal religion.	Imperfect religion.	The power of belief and wishes for perfection and ennoblement.	The power of conviction which allows us to believe in God, but due to insufficient self-cognition we do not recognize Him.
46.	We use whatever nature gives us in moderation.	Because of false doctrines we reject particular gifts of nature.	Power of the multifarious and goal-oriented development of mankind.	The power of ignorance and false and harmful asceticism.
47.	Maturity.	Immaturity.	The power of consciousness, of conviction and proper assessment of our magical development.	Ignorance of the level of development in self-cognition and magic.
48.	We do not interfere in future events regarding our own and someone else's fate. We live in the present.	We interfere in our future fate and that of someone else.	The power of knowledge and command of the universal laws, above all the karmic laws.	The power of curiosity and ignorance, and lack of control of the universal laws and above all the karmic laws.

	Active-Positive	Passive-Negative	Active-Positive	Passive-Negative
49.	Farsightedness.	Short-sightedness, delusion.	The power of knowledge and maturity, power of wisdom.	The power of ignorance, and striving for successes for egotistical reasons.
50.	Adaptability.	Inability to adapt.	The power of secrets, of silence, of harmony, of elasticity.	The power of our stubbornness that we use to disclose convictions and secrets. The power of disharmony, of inelasticity, of rigidity.
51.	Reservedness.	We do not have our feelings, thoughts, passions, and negative attributes under control. We lose our footing.	We seek security, certainty, and truth.	We are inclined toward impulsiveness and regret.
52.	Simplicity.	Complexity, confusion.	Power that is effective without support.	Undeveloped weak power, belief, and ability that requires support.
53.	Gracefulness, harmony, i.e. talent for eloquence etc.	Disharmony, i.e. not being able to speak coherently etc.	The power of beauty and art.	The power of ugliness of plagiarism, counterfeiting, etc.
54.	We do not avoid duties, beneficial restrictions, and asceticism.	We avoid duties, beneficial restrictions, and asceticism.	The power of duty and true asceticism.	The power of disgust toward duties and anything unpleasant, even when we have accepted that duty or task.
55.	Interest in self-cognition.	Disinterested in ennobling the spirit, soul and physical body.	The power of maturity for our ennoblement in all four elements and on all planes.	The power immaturity for self-cognition, of attachment to the material.

	Active-Positive	Passive-Negative	Active-Positive	Passive-Negative
56.	Wealth on all planes.	Yearning for material wealth, which is not necessary but harmful, and which does not agree with our development.	The power of perfection and noble-mindedness (magnanimity).	The power of yearning for and attaching ourselves to a material lifestyle, wealth, comfort, pleasure, gluttony, passions etc.
57.	We wish other people a long life and everything good.	We wish the death of another person for egotistical motives.	The power of true love for our fellowman.	The power of cruel egotism.
58.	We wish every person success, so that failure is followed by success.	Egotistical joy at the failure of other people.	The power of sympathizing with other people's failures and successes as if they were our own.	The power of schadenfreude, egotistical joy, about the failures of other people. These kinds of powers fall back on us.
59.	Contemplation, reflection.	We do not reflect or contemplate at all.	The power of peace and quiet and making the right decisions.	The power of jumping to conclusions without proper thinking.
60.	We condemn or judge ourselves, never someone else. We never malign another person.	Condemning and slandering other people.	The power of self-cognition, the knowledge and command of the karmic laws.	Power of the ignorance of the karmic laws in regards to judging our fellowman.
61.	Equanimity on the material plane.	Exaggerated worries about earthly matters.	The power of a clear self-cognition.	We cling to a material life and earthly possessions.
62.	We do not identify ourselves with the attributes of our fellowman. We isolate ourselves strictly from the infiltration of negative attributes.	We share the attributes of our fellowman and identify ourselves with him against our will.	The power of wisdom, of caution, and the protection of our equilibrium.	The power of carelessness, ignorance, and not being in command of the universal laws.

	Active-Positive	Passive-Negative	Active-Positive	Passive-Negative
63.	Complete honesty.	Hypocrisy.	The power of truth.	The power of falsehood, of distortion and self-praise.
64.	We always pay attention and are alert.	Fading alertness.	The power of defense toward the activities of passions and bad attributes.	Little interest in ennobling the spirit, soul and physical body.
65.	Respect for our fellowman and his religion.	No respect for our fellowman or his religion.	The knowledge and command of the universal laws.	The power of egotism, one-sidedness, force or violence against the particular convictions and activities of our fellowman.
66.	We do not underestimate ourselves or other people.	We underestimate ourselves as well as other people.	The power of true humility.	The power of weakness and ignorance in ourselves and others.
67.	Consideration for things which do not belong to us.	Theft.	We deal with other people's possessions properly.	We appropriate things we do not own.
68.	Proper behavior toward other people.	Primitive, bad, animalistic behavior.	The power of perfection, of ennoblement, of balance.	The power of uncontrollable passions.
69.	We follow all the instructions of the magical exercises precisely, punctually, and faithfully.	We do not follow the instructions during the exercises.	The power of systematics, of sense of duty, resolution (perseverance, diligence, patience).	The power of proceeding unsystematically, of being scatter-brained. We do not fulfill our duties and do not keep our resolutions (laziness, convenience, moodiness).
70.	Genuine true religion.	Egotistical religion.	Power of conviction and belief in a universal religion.	Power of egotism that draws material advantages from religion.

	Active-Positive	Passive-Negative	Active-Positive	Passive-Negative
71.	Honesty.	Dishonesty.	The power of honesty and justness.	The power of dishonesty and injustice.
72.	Proper asceticism.	Senseless renunciation, false asceticism.	The power that leads us to perfection and self-discipline.	The power of unreasonable and distorted asceticism that harms our health and possessions.
73.	Clear cognition of passing over from the material to the astral plane.	We resign ourselves to old age and death.	Power that severs the astral matrix from the physical body as a consequence of the disintegrating effects of the elements.	The power of ignorance, of despair and fear that everything has come to an end.
74.	We have control over everything that we do consciously.	Bad habits, quirks, involuntary movement etc.	We control all functions of the material and astral body.	The will has no power over various bad habits, quirks etc.
75.	Strong defense against anything harmful.	Weak defense against anything harmful.	The power of constant introspection.	The will is too weak to fight against what is harmful. We are controlled by passion and negative attributes.
76.	We are unwavering in our resolutions, word, promises, and vows (oath).	Deliberate disregard for resolutions and promises we have made etc.	The power of duty, honor, and lawfulness.	The power of carelessness, of betrayal, conscious disregard of our promises.
77.	We are enthused about our compulsory exercises to which we have committed ourselves.	Reluctance to exercise, to train.	The power of enthusiasm for the ennoblement of the spirit, the soul and the physical body in order to reach the highest goal.	Power of laziness, lack of enthusiasm and apathy in doing our exercises, which we only do for egotistical reasons.
78.	Astuteness, perspicacity, agility (Air element).	Ponderousness, clumsiness, apathy.	The power of intelligence, of the intellect, of skillfulness, quickness and cheerfulness.	We need a long time to comprehend, to perceive, to react.

	Active-Positive	Passive-Negative	Active-Positive	Passive-Negative
79.	Joy of life.	Despair.	Basic equilibrium.	Power of severe melancholy that eats away at a person until he or she commits suicide.
80.	Helpfulness, prepared to act, etc.	We are unprepared to set something into motion, to help etc.	The power of sympathy.	The power of antipathy.
81.	Magnanimity.	Faint-heartedness.	The power of ennoblement, chivalry.	Power of bias, prejudice, miserliness, stinginess.
82.	Friendliness.	Envy.	Power of sympathy.	Power of antipathy.
83.	We reject no one, we condemn no one.	Hidden and open joy in the condemnation and judgment of others.	The power of knowledge and being in command of the laws of karma.	The power that rejects and condemns other people with joy.
84.	Everything is pure, even the eliminatory organs and excrement.	The feeling that the physical body, the physical, the carnal is unclean.	The power of purity in everything created.	Power of impurity. Certain substances are considered impure, even from the magical, hermetic viewpoint.
85.	We reject any kind of reward.	We expect rewards (remuneration).	The power of unselfishness.	We expect a reward for helping others (e.g. like trained animals receive a treat).
86.	Respecting one's personal space. We do not harm other people.	Deliberate harm to others in thoughts, feelings and actions.	The power of love and respectfulness of other people in a passive respect.	The power of hate, egotistical use of force.
87.	Reliability of the senses.	Loss of orientation.	We can orient ourselves at all times, we know the time of day etc.	Bad sense of orientation; great difficulty estimating height, distance etc. caused by a malfunction of our senses and consciousness.

	Active-Positive	Passive-Negative	Active-Positive	Passive-Negative
88.	We desire nothing that threatens the existence of another human being.	For selfish reasons we wish to have the professional position held by another person.	The power of the conscience and true love.	The power of egotism that does not respect the well-being of other people.
89.	We fulfill our own needs within the limits of our possibilities.	Exaggerated thriftiness.	The power of appropriateness, keeping within the limits.	The power of exaggerated stinginess, miserliness.
90.	Indifference to things that do not concern us.	We react to the trivial remarks of other people.	The power of indifference wherever it is appropriate or when it applies.	The power of curiosity, talkativeness (gossip), insignificance.
91.	Genuine joy at everything that happens to us, whether positive or negative.	False joy that we can live so long in the physical world. False joy on the whole.	The power of honesty, of self-cognition and the recognition of everything outside ourselves.	The power of false, insincere optimism which originates from a selfish viewpoint.
92.	We fulfill our duties punctually.	We are always behind with our work.	Power of our conscience. We fulfill our duties under any circumstances.	Power of disharmony, of disorder and naughtiness. No sense of duty.
93.	Obedience, wherever it is appropriate.	Disobedience where not appropriate, i.e. we do not obey when we are duty-bound to do so.	We follow the order of our conscience, of intuition and inspiration.	The power of defiance, of stubbornness, pigheadedness, rage, insult, envy which force us to ignore the voice of our conscience.
94.	Purity in everything and everywhere.	Dubious purity of the physical body and thoughts.	The power of absolute perfection.	We adhere to a false conviction that there is something impure from a universal viewpoint.
95.	Truthfulness, reality, truth.	Lies, falsehood.	The power of absolute truth.	The power of lies.
96.	Justness, unselfishness.	We are calculating.	We have no selfish interests.	We have selfish interests.

	Active-Positive	Passive-Negative	Active-Positive	Passive-Negative
97.	Determination, certainty, confidence.	Undecidedness, slowness.	The power of conviction and confidence in personal abilities.	The power of insecurity and distrust in our abilities.
98.	Passions that are under control (negative attributes).	Uncontrolled and unsatisfied passions.	The power of the intellect and the will.	The power of suppressed passions.
99.	We always reach those goals for which our powers are sufficient.	Inability, impotence.	The correct assessment of our own abilities and powers.	The power that makes an effort in vain to attain something for which our powers are not sufficient.
100.	Foresight, farsightedness.	Thoughtlessness, rashness.	The power of the intellect, of intelligence that clearly recognizes the causes and the consequences.	The power of ignorance; we do not pay attention to the causal law.
101.	We are open and honest, and admit our mistakes.	We hide from our bad conscience.	The power of conscience.	We fear the consequence of a bad conscience.
102.	Perfection, completion.	Materialism, one-sidedness.	The power of perfection and being in command of the universal laws.	The power of one-sidedness, of imperfection.
103.	Adaptability.	Insufficient adaptability.	The power of silence.	We disclose what we do not agree with; we profane ourselves.
104.	Honesty, directness.	Hypocrisy, falsehood.	The power of a clear conscience, humility.	The power of lies, hypocrisy, dishonesty and self-praise.
105.	Reality.	Fantasy.	The power of truth.	Power of transitory reality.
106.	Sympathy and help.	Cynicism toward someone in need.	The power of mercy and love for our fellowman.	The power of cruel heartlessness.

	Active-Positive	Passive-Negative	Active-Positive	Passive-Negative
107.	Peace and contentment no matter if we are facing something positive or negative. Everything is important from an educational viewpoint.	Bitterness.	The power of clear self-cognition and knowledge of the universal laws.	We do not know the educational effects of negative attributes, and we do not trust them.
108.	Overabundance of everything that we require for a balanced lifestyle.	Poverty, misery.	Equilibrium of the elements on all planes.	Malfunction of some of the elements that are active in a human being.
109.	Sense of duty and everything that makes a good character.	Carelessness.	The power of good habits that we keep for our entire lives.	The power of carelessness and recklessness that prevents us from fulfilling our duties and developing good habits.
110.	Fearlessness.	Shyness, timidity.	We look at everyone directly and openly and we do not conceal anything that is considered natural.	Unfounded fear of other people; we hide our character, and suppress our self-expression.
111.	Peacefulness.	Gruffness.	The power that serves the purpose of dealing with difficult matters in a peaceful manner.	The power of unyieldingness when it comes to solving particular problems between people.
112.	Flexibility, progressiveness.	Stiffness, rigidity, conservative position or outlook.	The power of evolution.	The power that is attached to tradition that stops our progress.
113.	Competence, ability.	Laziness.	Positive power of the elements of Fire, Air and Earth.	Power of dependency on the work of other people.
114.	Directness, honesty.	Cunningness.	Power of truth.	Power of lies, of egotism, dishonesty and thinking for our advantage.

	Active-Positive	Passive-Negative	Active-Positive	Passive-Negative
115.	Forgiveness, mercy.	Unyieldingness, unmerciful, unforgiving, hard-heartedness.	Power of cognition of true causes, power of leniency and true love.	The power of cruel egotism and stinginess.
116.	Independence.	Stereotyping.	The power of knowledge and the will.	We meticulously follow imperfect rules.
117.	Complete openness and honesty without any hidden negative intentions.	Underhandedness, insidiousness.	The power of a clear conscience.	We have a friendly expression on our face, yet our true intentions are hostile.
118.	Proper caution.	Exaggerated caution.	The power that protects us from everything harmful, so that we do not do anything evil.	Power of overstated caution entices us and prevents us from helping someone because of possible harm to self.
119.	Endurance, perseverance.	Weariness.	The power of the will.	Power of a weak will which is controlled by an uncontrolled spirit; fickleness.
120.	Willingness to sacrifice.	Unwillingness to sacrifice.	The power of mercy.	The power of egotism, of heartlessness and toughness.
121.	We would like to recognize ourselves.	No interest in self-cognition.	The power of introspection, of self-cognition, desire for knowledge, for differentiation and recognition.	The power of imperfection, of immaturity.
122.	Wealth.	Poverty.	The power of the equilibrium of the elements which endows a person with all kinds of wealth in the amount that corresponds with his level of development.	The power that causes and determines any lack in the life of an incomplete person.

	Active-Positive	Passive-Negative	Active-Positive	Passive-Negative
123.	We keep silent about our own authority in the presence of the uninitiated.	We make an effort to be respected and be in authority.	The power of silence.	The power of our own nothingness and vanity (emptiness). Efforts to gain pomp and circumstance.
124.	Not touching things that do not belong to us.	Stealthiness, pilfering, adorning ourselves with borrowed finery.	The power of absolute justness.	The power of passions; we acquire other people's possessions (through theft).
125.	We disguise our true character in the presence of the uninitiated through silence.	We exhibit our own individuality and yearn for personal importance.	The power of silence.	The power that yearns for acknowledgement, praise, importance and recognition.
126.	Punctuality, consequence.	Apologies, excuses, carelessness.	The power of resolutions, of promises and carrying out our duties, come what may.	Weak resolutions, we do not carry out our duties and do not keep our word.
127.	Normal consciousness.	Senseless circumstances.	The power of a balanced intellect, the power of the tetrapolar magnet.	The power of the uncontrollable effect of the subconscious.
128.	Lawfulness, systematics.	Chaos.	The power of the universal law of harmony.	The power of disruption, of disharmony, mistakes and unlawfulness.
129.	Discretion, silence.	Profanity, talkativeness.	The power of silence, of discretion.	The power of showing-off in the presence of the uninitiated.

Titles By and About Franz Bardon

The series of books on Hermetics (Alchemy) by Franz Bardon reveals the Holy Mysteries. They are unique in that they contain theory and practice. It is important that these works be read and practiced in the proper sequence. Should the reader not do so, he will have great difficulties in understanding the content, even from a philosophical view point; as for the practitioner, he will not progress at all. Therefore, it is advisable for everyone to follow this sequence:

Frabato the Magician (introduction)
Initiation into Hermetics (Vol. I)
The Practice of Magical Evocation (Vol. II)
The Key to the True Kabbalah (Vol. III)
Franz Bardon: Questions & Answers — The Great Arcanum
Memories of Franz Bardon
The Universal Master Key

Other Titles By Merkur Publishing, Inc.

The Great Gospel of John (6 volumes)
The Lord's Sermons
Saturn
Earth & Moon
The Advent of Christ
The Healing Power of Sunlight
The Lord's Book of Life & Health
Alchemy Unveiled
Seven Hermetic Letters
Philosophia Mystica: The Prophecies of the Prophet Daniel
Magic: Principles of Higher Knowledge
Scandals in the Roman Catholic Church
Becoming the Lotus (How to Master the Full Lotus Posture)
How to Develop Your Occult Powers